Understanding Geography

Map Skills and Our World

Level 3

©2018 Maps.com, 120 Cremona Drive, Suite 260, Santa Barbara, CA 93117 / 805-685-3100

ISBN 978-1-930194-21-2

Visit the world's premier map website at http://www.maps.com for thousands of map resources, including driving directions, address finding, and downloadable maps.

Table of Contents

Key Words: globe, map, satellite image, continent, ocean

A globe

To learn about the Earth, two of the best tools you can use are **globes** and **maps**. Sometimes, it's better to use a globe. Other times, a map works better.

Globes

A globe is a model of the planet Earth. If you went into outer space, the Earth would look like a globe. Like the Earth, a globe is round. Most globes are tilted a little to one side. This is how the Earth looks in space when it circles around the sun.

Globes show **continents** and **oceans**. A continent is a very large area of land. There are seven continents on Earth. An ocean is a huge body of salt water. There are five oceans on Earth.

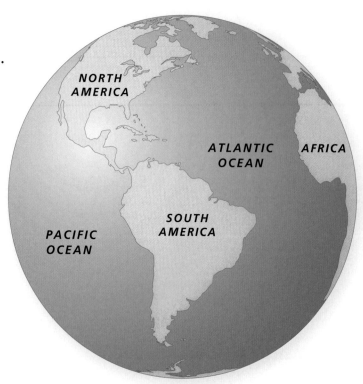

Look at the picture just above. It shows part of a globe.

1. Can you see the whole Earth, or just half of the Earth?

2. North America is one of the seven continents. Name two other continents you see on the globe.

3. The Pacific Ocean is one of the five oceans. Name one other ocean you see on the globe.

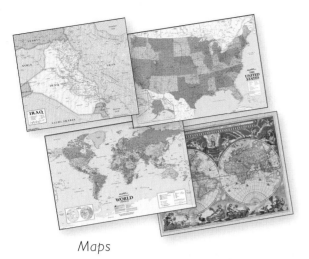

Maps

Maps

You can find maps in many places, such as in books, on classroom walls, and even on T-shirts. Like globes, world maps show the Earth's oceans and continents. Maps are flat. You can fold some maps and carry them with you.

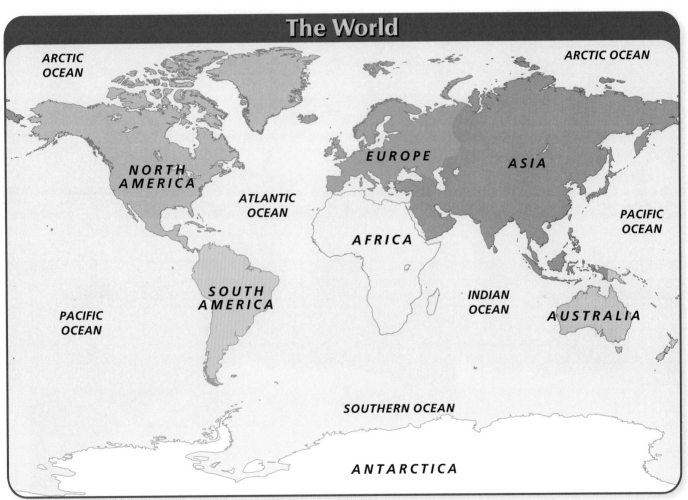

This world map shows the Earth's seven continents and five oceans.

4. Find each of the seven continents on the map: North America, South America, Europe, Asia, Africa, Australia, and Antarctica.

5. Find each of these oceans on the map: the Atlantic Ocean, Pacific Ocean, Indian Ocean, Arctic Ocean, and Southern Ocean.

6. Which continents and oceans do you see on both this map and the globe on the opposite page?

Satellite Images

This picture is a **satellite image**. It is a photograph taken by a satellite orbiting the Earth. A satellite is a small spaceship. As the satellites circle around the Earth, they sometimes take pictures. On this satellite image, you can see land, water, and clouds.

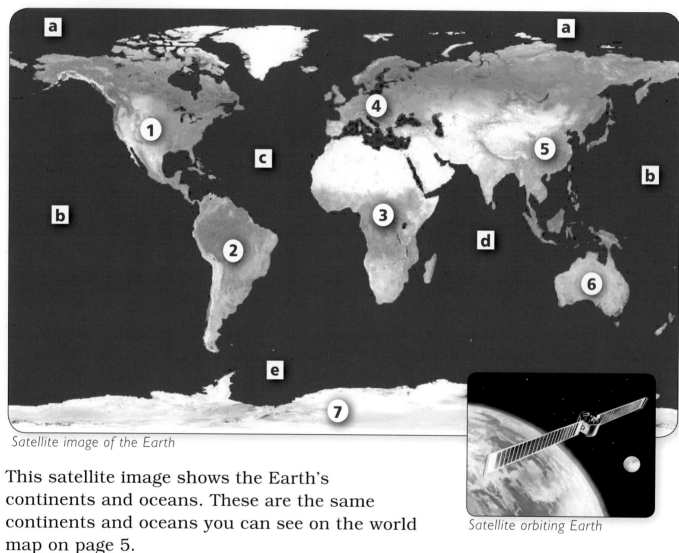

Satellite image of the Earth

Satellite orbiting Earth

This satellite image shows the Earth's continents and oceans. These are the same continents and oceans you can see on the world map on page 5.

Look at the numbers and letters on this satellite image. The continents have numbers. The oceans have letters.

7. Match the numbers above with the following continents: Asia, Africa, Antarctica, Australia, Europe, North America, South America.

8. Match the letters above with the following oceans: Atlantic, Arctic, Indian, Pacific, Southern.

The globe on the left and the satellite image on the right show the exact same area of the Earth.

9. Name the five continents you see on the globe and satellite image.

10. Look at this globe and satellite image. Then look at the world map on page 5. Which continents do you see on the world map but not on the globe and satellite image?

11. Name the largest body of water you see on the globe and satellite image.

Skill Builder

Review

1. Name one difference between a globe and a map.
2. True or False: A globe is a model of the planet Earth.
3. True or False: A continent is a large body of water.

Try It Yourself

Cut 11 small pieces of paper. Write the names of the seven continents and five oceans, one name on each piece. Fold the pieces and put them in a box. Pull out one piece and read the name. Then find that continent or ocean on a world map or globe. Take turns with a friend, or find all 12 yourself.

Activity 2 Map Keys

Key Words: map key, locator map

Have you ever seen a star or a dot on a map? A **map key** tells you what those symbols mean. For example, the map key might tell you that a dot stands for a city, or that the color green indicates flat, grassy areas called plains. You can usually find the map key in a box near the edge of the map.

Look at the map below. It has a small map set inside it. This small map shows the United States, with the state of Colorado highlighted in red. This small map is called a **locator map**. A locator map shows the location of a place in a country or the world.

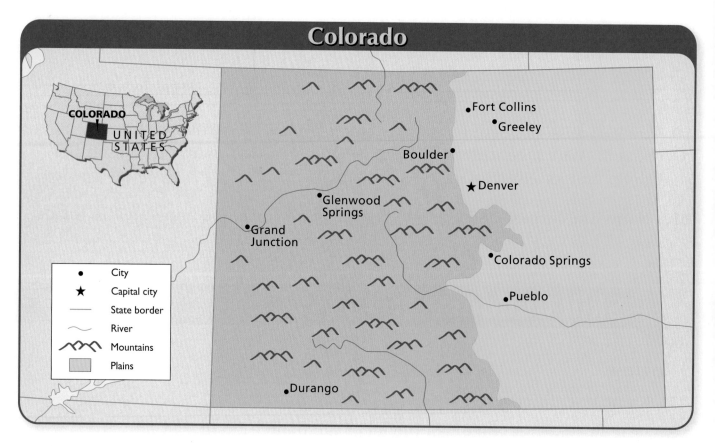

Colorado

- • City
- ★ Capital city
- — State border
- ～ River
- ⋀⋀⋀ Mountains
- ▢ Plains

Look at this map of Colorado. Then look at the map key.

1. Find the mountains on the map key and then find the mountains on the map.

2. Find the plains on the map key and then point to the plains on the map.

3. What do the small dots stand for?

4. Which city is the capital of Colorado? Find it on the map.

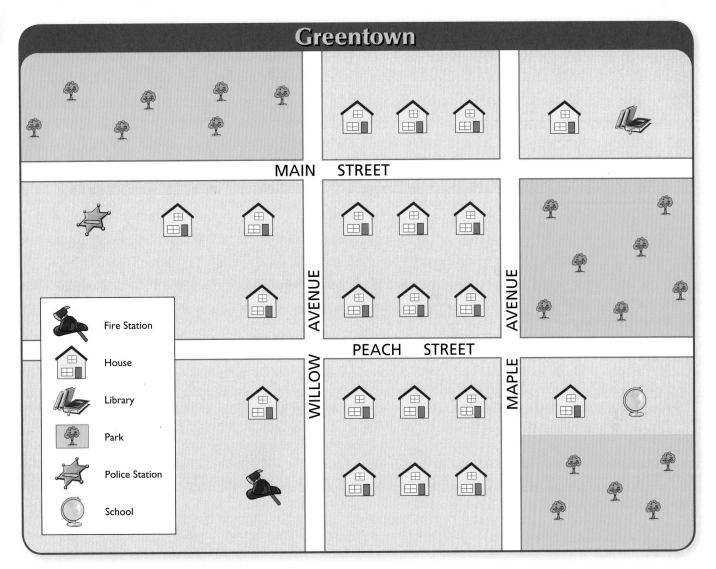

This is a map of a small town called Greentown. The map shows buildings you usually find in a town, like houses and schools. It also shows parks and some of the town's services, like the police station, the fire station, and the library.

First look at the map key. Then find the buildings and other places on the map.

5. What is the symbol for a park?

6. What is the symbol for a library?

7. How many houses are on Main Street between Willow Avenue and Maple Avenue?

8. On what street is the school located?

9. On what street is the police station located?

10. On what street is the fire station located?

The map below shows you the country of Italy, highlighted in green. Notice how it is shaped like a boot. Italy is in Europe. The small locator globe shows Italy in red. When people travel to Italy, they visit beautiful old buildings. They see museums with famous paintings. They enjoy Italian food and Italy's beautiful countryside.

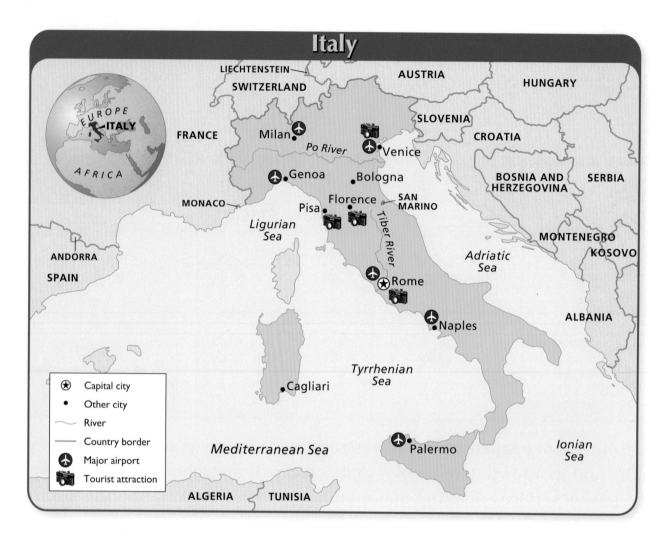

The map shows some of Italy's most famous cities. Use the map key to help you answer the following questions.

11. What city is the capital of Italy?

12. Name two cities in Italy that are close to major airports.

13. Name two cities in Italy that do not have large airports.

14. Name two rivers in Italy.

15. Name one country that is next to Italy.

16. Is the city of Venice a tourist attraction? How can you tell?

Pisa and Venice are two famous cities in Italy. People visit Pisa to see its Leaning Tower. Venice is fun because it has canals running right through the city. People travel in special boats called gondolas.

Leaning Tower of Pisa

Venice, Italy

17. Find Pisa and Venice on the map of Italy.

18. Pretend it's your job to make new symbols on the map. Look at the photographs of Pisa and Venice. Then decide what symbols you would draw for each city.

Skill Builder

Review

1. True or False: A map key shows you what the symbols on a map stand for.

2. On the map of Italy, what is the symbol for a tourist attraction?

3. On the map of Italy, what symbol shows a city?

Try It Yourself

Draw a map of your bedroom on a sheet of paper. First, draw lines for the walls. Then think of a symbol for a door, and draw that symbol in the places in your bedroom that have doors. Think of another symbol for a window. Add that symbol to the map to show where the room has windows. Add other symbols for your bed and one other thing in your room. Make a map key showing what the symbols on the map mean.

Cardinal Directions

Imagine that you ask a friend for directions to the movie theater. She tells you to go two blocks to the west. Do you know where to go?

It's important to know your directions. On most maps, a **compass rose** shows the directions north, east, south, and west. These are called the **cardinal directions**. On the compass rose below, N means north, E means east, S means south, and W means west.

Touch the middle of the compass rose below. Then move your finger to the right. Which direction did you move your finger? Move your finger back to the middle and then down. Now which direction is your finger going?

A compass can help you find your way.

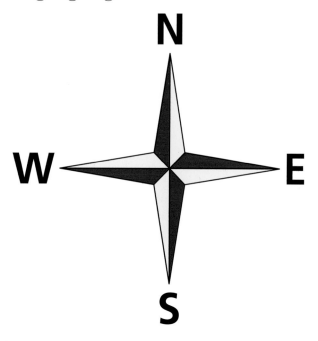

The next time you go outside, stand and face north. You can use a compass like the one above to help you find north. The needle on a compass always points north. If you don't have a compass to show you which way is north, ask an adult to help you. As you face north, spread your arms out wide. Your right arm is pointing east.

1. Which way is your left arm pointing?

2. Which direction is behind your back?

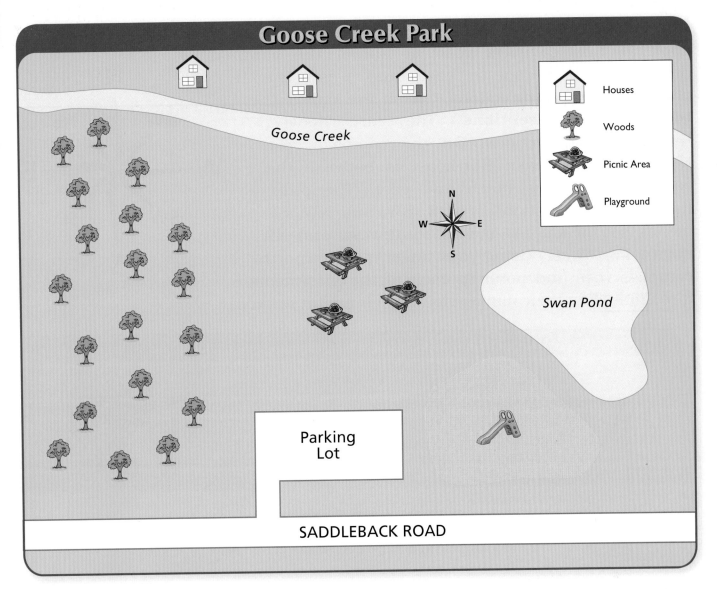

Goose Creek Park

Imagine that you visit Goose Creek Park. You can have all sorts of fun at the park. You can go to the playground. You can have a picnic. You can go for a walk in the woods.

Look at the map of Goose Creek Park. Point to the compass rose. Use the compass rose to help you answer the following questions.

3. Is north at the top of the map or bottom of the map?

4. If you have finished your picnic and want to walk to the woods, which direction should you go?

5. Is Swan Pond east or west of the picnic area?

6. What road will you come to if you walk south from Goose Creek?

7. Is the playground east or west of the parking lot?

8. What is north of Goose Creek?

Intermediate Directions

Look at this compass rose. It shows the cardinal directions—north, south, east, and west. But it also shows more directions. These are called the **intermediate directions**. They are between the cardinal directions. On the compass rose NE means northeast. Northeast is between the cardinal directions north and east. The other intermediate directions are SE, SW, and NW. SE means southeast, SW means southwest, and NW means northwest. Using your finger, go around the compass rose and point to each of the intermediate directions. Say their names aloud as you point to them.

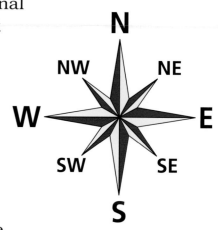

The map above shows part of the United States. Find Ohio and North Dakota on the map. North Dakota is northwest of Ohio. Ohio is southeast of North Dakota.

9. Name two states southeast of North Dakota.

10. Name two states northeast of Kansas.

11. Name two states southwest of Michigan.

12. What direction would you travel to go from Wisconsin to Nebraska?

13. What direction would you travel to go from Indiana to Minnesota?

Find Illinois on the Midwest United States map. Then look at this map of Illinois. Find the compass rose on the map.

14. Which city is farther north, Springfield or Chicago?

15. Which city is farther east, Decatur or Quincy?

16. Name two cities southwest of Evanston.

17. Name two cities northwest of Carbondale.

18. In what direction would you travel to get from the city of Quincy to Lake Michigan?

Skill Builder

Review

1. Why is it important to know your directions?

2. What are the four cardinal directions?

3. Name the four intermediate directions.

Try It Yourself

Use the U.S. political map on pages 70–71 to help you with the following activities:

Find your state on the United States map. Figure out which directions you would travel in order to visit these states: Michigan, Washington, Arizona, Delaware, Georgia, and Kansas.

You are going on a road trip of the United States. You start and finish your trip in Washington, D.C. You will first visit the city of Jackson, Mississippi. Next you will drive to Portland, Oregon. After this you will travel to Minneapolis, Minnesota, and then to Nashville, Tennessee. Finally you will return to Washington, D.C. Write down the directions you would travel between each of the cities on your tour.

Key words: equator, prime meridian, North Pole, South Pole, hemisphere

Equator and Prime Meridian

Have you ever wondered why there are lines on maps and globes? Do you think you could see any of these lines on Earth? The answer is no. You can't see any of these lines on Earth. They are imaginary lines. But these lines are very useful on maps and globes. One of the most important imaginary lines is called the **equator**. This line goes around the middle of the Earth. Find the equator on the world map.

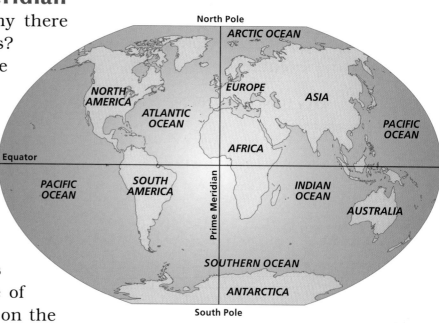

Many places at the equator are very hot. The sun shines directly onto the equator for twelve hours every day, all year round.

The Earth has another important imaginary line. This line goes from north to south. It's called the **prime meridian**. Find the prime meridian on the world map.

Here is a warm place near the Equator.

Places near the poles are very cold.

The Poles

Imagine a place that never gets warm. If you went there, you might shiver all the time. This is what it's like at the Earth's poles. The Earth has two poles. The **North Pole** is as far north as you can go on Earth. The **South Pole** is as far as you can go south. The poles are cold because they don't get much direct sunlight.

16

Northern and Southern Hemispheres

If you were to slice the Earth along the equator, you would end up with two halves. Each half is called a **hemisphere**. "Hemi" means half. Everything south of the equator is in the Southern Hemisphere. Everything north of the equator is in the Northern Hemisphere.

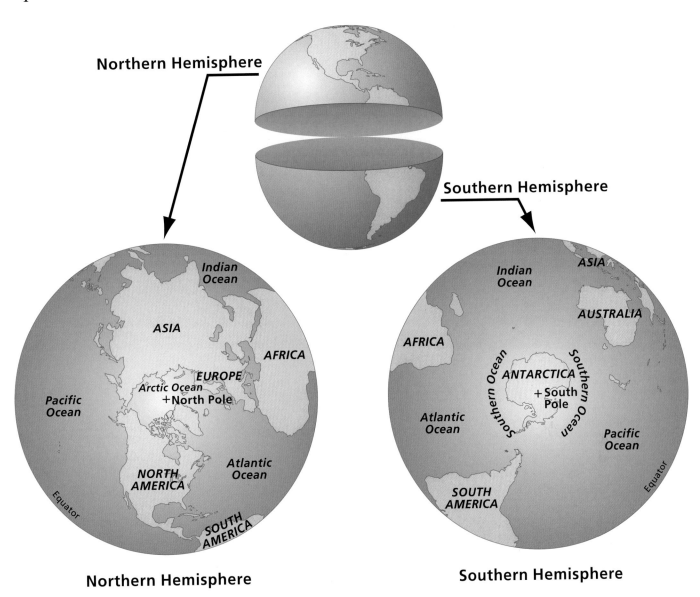

Northern Hemisphere

Southern Hemisphere

Look at the maps above. The map on the left shows what the Northern Hemisphere looks like from the North Pole. The map on the right shows what the Southern Hemisphere looks like from the South Pole.

1. Is North America in the Northern Hemisphere or Southern Hemisphere?

2. Is Australia in the Northern Hemisphere or the Southern Hemisphere?

3. Is Africa in the Northern Hemisphere or Southern Hemisphere or both?

4. In which hemisphere is the Arctic Ocean located? What three oceans are located in both the Northern and Southern Hemispheres?

Eastern and Western Hemispheres

If you were to slice the Earth along the prime meridian you would end up with two halves, the Eastern Hemisphere and the Western Hemisphere. Everything east of the prime meridian is in the Eastern Hemisphere. Everything west of the prime meridian is in the Western Hemisphere.

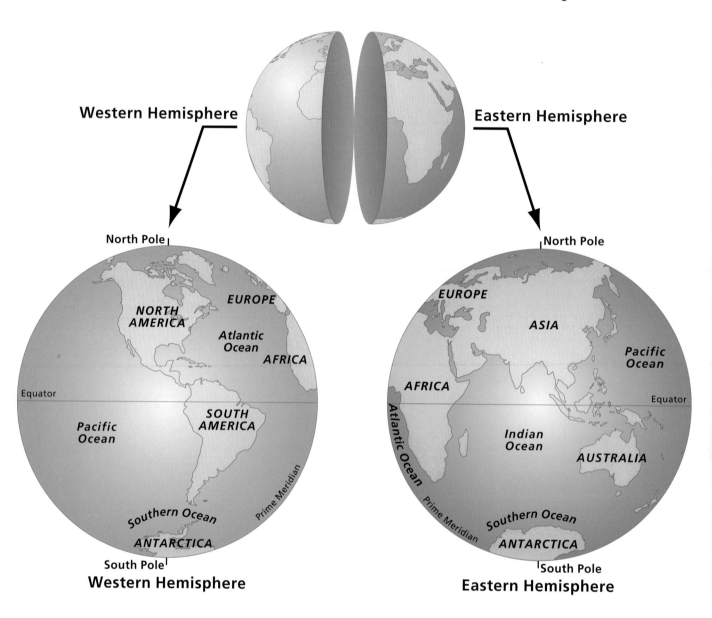

Look at the maps above. The map on the left shows the Western Hemisphere. The map on the right shows the Eastern Hemisphere.

5. Which two continents are located only in the Western Hemisphere?

6. Is Asia located in the Eastern Hemisphere or the Western Hemisphere?

7. Which oceans are located in the Western Hemisphere?

8. Which oceans are located in the Eastern Hemisphere?

Every continent is in at least two hemispheres. For example, Asia is in the Northern Hemisphere and the Eastern Hemisphere.

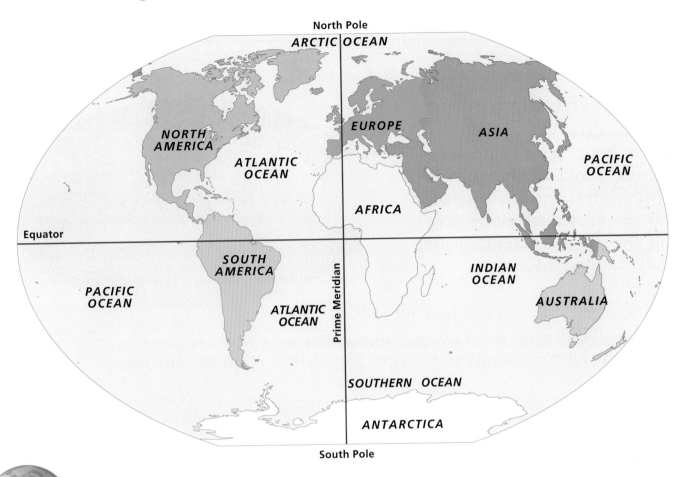

Skill Builder

Review

1. Which three continents does the equator cross?
2. Which three continents does the prime meridian cross?
3. Is the Arctic Ocean in the Northern Hemisphere or Southern Hemisphere?
4. In which two hemispheres is Australia located?
5. In which two hemispheres is most of South America located?
6. Which continent is closer to the North Pole, Africa or Europe?
7. Which continent is closer to the South Pole, South America or Asia?

Try It Yourself

Pretend you're planning to travel to the Northern and Eastern Hemispheres. Name four countries you would visit. Use the political world map on pages 66–67 to choose the countries. Trace a line with your finger to show your route.

Key Words: neighborhood, community

Parts of the Planet

Imagine you can visit outer space. Your space ship takes you to another planet. You meet some friendly aliens. One of them asks you where you live. You respond, "I am from the planet Earth."

Now imagine that you've just moved to a new home in another state. You make a new friend. He asks you where you came from. What do you say?

You probably would not say you are from the planet Earth! Instead, you would name the city and the state you moved from.

We all live on planet Earth. To locate where we are on Earth, it helps to focus on parts of the planet. We can look at big parts, such as continents and countries.

We can also look at smaller parts. For example, in the United States, many people live in different states, cities, and towns. In cities and towns, many people live in a **neighborhood**.

Look at the globe. The biggest pieces of land on Earth are called continents. Do you live on the continent of North America?

1. Name the other continent you see on the globe.

2. Name the three oceans you see on the globe.

20

Many Countries

You can zoom in on a map to get closer and closer to your home or to another place. The map below shows part of the world. It zooms in on the continent of North America.

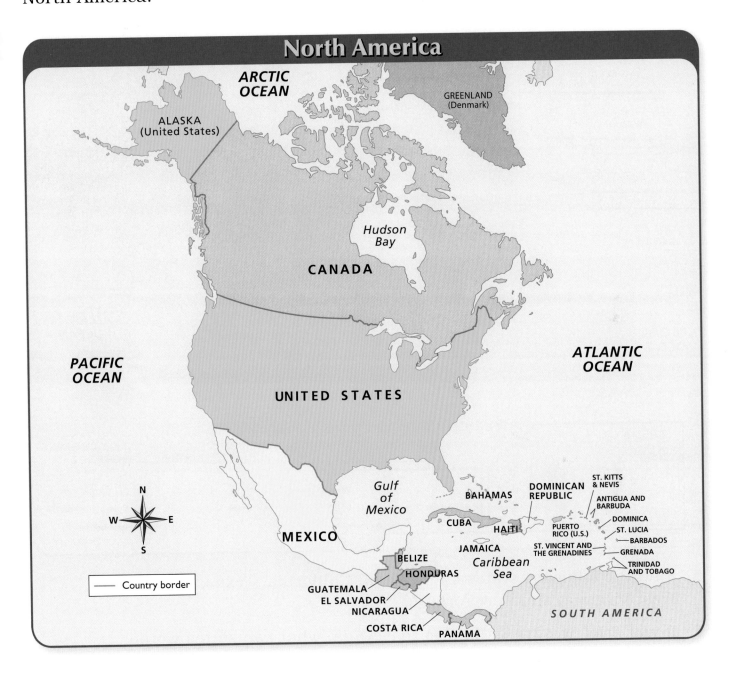

On the continent of North America, you can find different countries. The United States is one country.

3. What is the country just to the north of the United States?

4. Name two countries south of the United States.

You have just located several countries. Did you know that there are almost 200 different countries on Earth?

Many States

Our country, the United States, is divided into smaller parts, called states. There are 50 states.

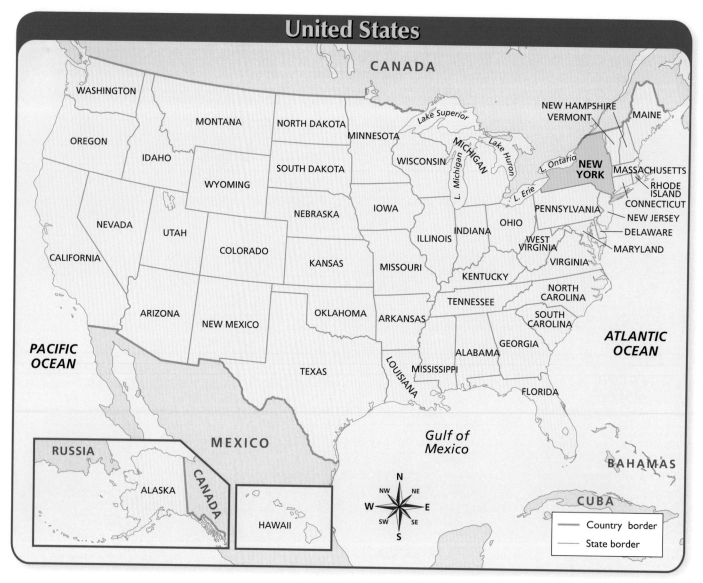

5. Find the following states on the map: California, Texas, Wisconsin, West Virginia, and New York.

6. If you drive west from Kansas to Nevada, what two states would you pass through?

7. What is the state directly north of Arkansas?

8. Name the state south of Georgia.

9. Name two states northwest of Utah.

10. Name two states that touch the Pacific Ocean.

11. Which state touches the Gulf of Mexico, Louisiana or Montana?

12. Which state is near the middle of the United States, Pennsylvania or Iowa?

One State

New York is a state in the northeastern part of the United States. New York City, the biggest city in the United States, is in the state of New York.

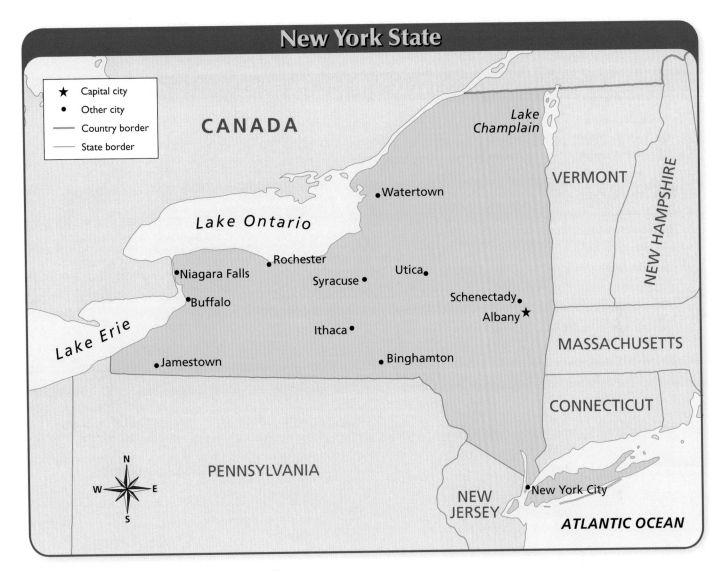

13. Is New York City located in the eastern or western part of New York State?

14. Name two other cities in the state of New York.

15. Name one lake that touches New York.

16. Name the two states south of New York.

17. What country is north of New York?

18. What direction would you drive to go from Syracuse to Niagara Falls?

19. What city is the capital of New York?

20. Name two states east of New York.

One City

Let's zoom in closer on the map and look at the city of New York. New York City has many tall skyscrapers. One of these skyscrapers is the Empire State Building. The city is divided into five parts called boroughs. The names of the boroughs are The Bronx, Brooklyn, Manhattan, Queens, and Staten Island. Try to find these five boroughs on the map

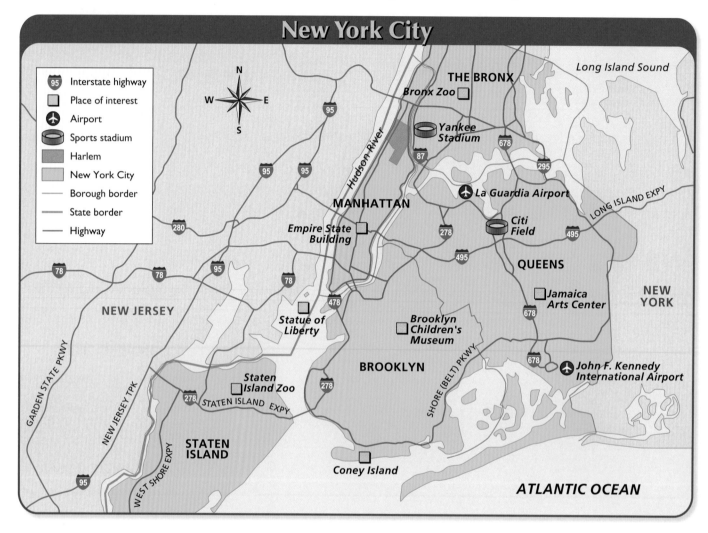

21. The Empire State Building is an interesting place to visit in New York City. Name two more places you could visit in the city.

22. Find two major airports in the city. What are they named?

23. What are the names of two big sports stadiums?

24. What do the red lines on the map show?

25. In which borough would you find Coney Island?

One Neighborhood

All cities have neighborhoods. A **neighborhood** is an area where people live near each other. New York has many neighborhoods. One is called Harlem. Use the map key to help you find Harlem on the map above.

One Community

Let's zoom in even closer. Now you can see Harlem. Harlem is a neighborhood of New York City that is famous for its jazz music.

Harlem is also a community. A **community** is a place where people live or work and do some of the same things together. Children in a community might go to the same school. Families in a community might eat at the same restaurants. They also use the library and parks. Some people may work in the same community in which they live.

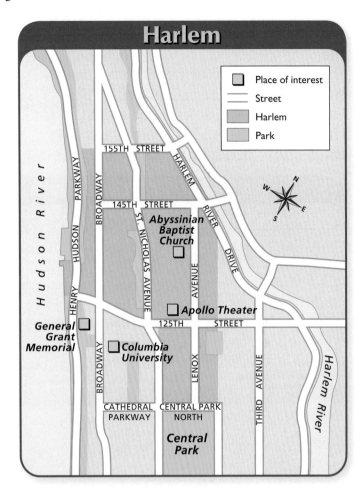

26. Name two streets in Harlem.

27. Name two buildings on the map.

28. On which street is the Apollo Theater located?

Skill Builder

Review

1. On which continent do you live?

2. In what country do you live?

3. Is South America a continent or a country?

4. Name three countries on the continent of North America.

5. What are some of your favorite places in your community?

Try It Yourself

Where do you live? "Zoom in" on your location. From bigger to smaller, list the following: your planet, continent, country, state, city or town, and street or road.

Activity 6 Countries, States, and Borders

Key Words: capital, political map, border

Have you ever wondered why maps have many different colors? They can be nice to look at, but that's not the only reason. The colors on this map show different countries. The colors make it easy for you to tell one country from another. You can see some of the country names on this map. One country you are familiar with is the United States.

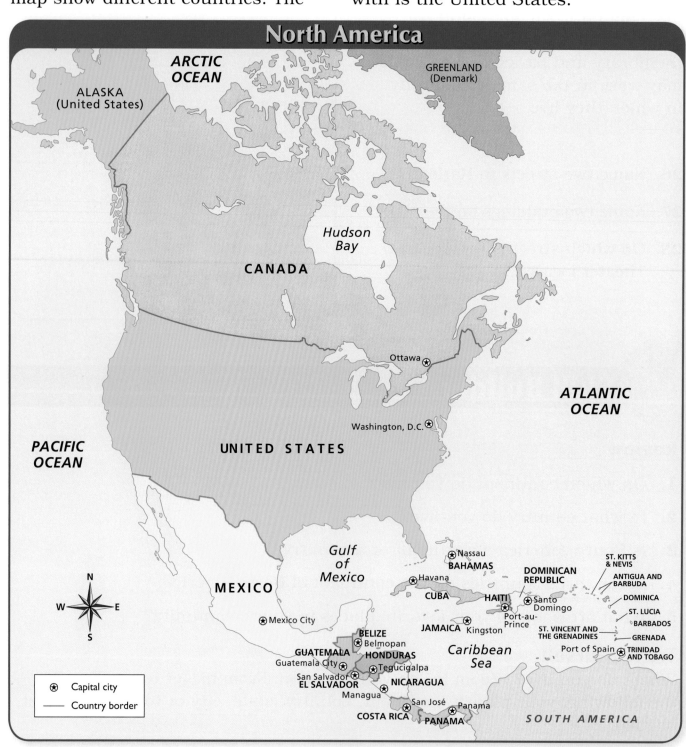

North America

ARCTIC OCEAN

GREENLAND (Denmark)

ALASKA (United States)

Hudson Bay

CANADA

Ottawa ⊛

ATLANTIC OCEAN

PACIFIC OCEAN

Washington, D.C. ⊛

UNITED STATES

Gulf of Mexico

⊛ Nassau
BAHAMAS

ST. KITTS & NEVIS

DOMINICAN REPUBLIC

ANTIGUA AND BARBUDA

⊛ Havana

DOMINICA

MEXICO

CUBA

HAITI

ST. LUCIA

⊛ Mexico City

JAMAICA

Santo Domingo

Port-au-Prince

BARBADOS

⊛ Kingston

ST. VINCENT AND THE GRENADINES

GRENADA

BELIZE

⊛ Belmopan

Caribbean Sea

Port of Spain ⊛ TRINIDAD AND TOBAGO

GUATEMALA

HONDURAS

Guatemala City ⊛

⊛ Tegucigalpa

San Salvador ⊛

NICARAGUA

EL SALVADOR

Managua ⊛

San José ⊛ Panama

COSTA RICA

PANAMA

SOUTH AMERICA

⊛ Capital city
— Country border

26

The U.S. Capitol building in Washington, D.C., the capital of the United States. Notice that you spell capitol, *the building where lawmakers meet, with an "o," but* capital, *the city, with an "a."*

The map also shows some of the **capital** cities. Capital cities are the places where government officials meet and work. The capital of the United States is Washington, D.C. On most maps the symbol for a capital city is a star.

The map of North America to the left is called a **political map**. Political maps show countries. They sometimes show states and cities, too. On a political map, you will see thin lines separating different countries and states. These lines are called **borders** or boundaries. Borders show where one country or state ends and another begins. The lines are only on the map—they are imaginary. If you step from Canada into the United States, you will not see a line on the ground.

Look at the map of North America.

1. Name the capitals of these countries: Canada, Mexico, and Cuba.

2. What two countries border Nicaragua?

3. Name a country that borders the Atlantic Ocean.

4. Name two countries that lie between the Caribbean Sea and the Pacific Ocean.

5. With what country does the state of Alaska share a border?

6. The Gulf of Mexico forms part of the border of two large countries. Name these two countries.

United States

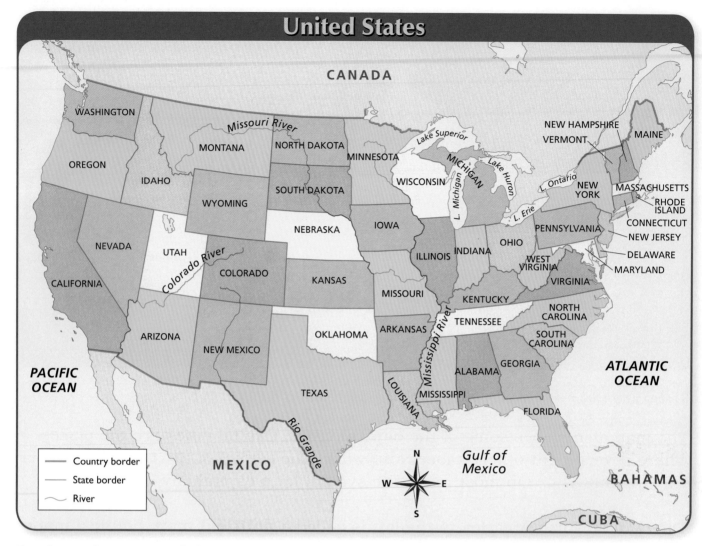

Look at this map of the United States. The map shows state and country borders. Can you see that some borders are straight and some borders are not straight at all?

Sometimes states or countries are separated by physical features, such as a river or a mountain range. Oceans and lakes can form borders, too. Physical features usually form borders that are not straight. Most straight borders were marked off by people.

7. Name two states that border Utah. Do you think their borders with Utah are formed by physical features or were marked off by people? Why?

8. What body of water borders California to the west?

9. What physical feature separates Nebraska and Iowa?

10. Name two states with a border on the Mississippi River.

11. What type of physical feature forms a border between the state of Michigan and the country of Canada?

28

Mexico is the country to the south of the United States. A river called the Río Grande forms part of the border between these two countries. The Río Grande begins in Colorado. It first flows south. Then it flows southeast until it reaches the Gulf of Mexico.

12. Trace the path of the Río Grande from Colorado to the Gulf of Mexico. What states does the Río Grande go through?

13. What four states are on the border with Mexico?

Skill Builder

Review

1. True or False: Capital cities are places where government officials meet and work.

2. What information does a political map show?

3. Name the landscape feature that is on the border between Iowa and Illinois.

Use the political world map on pages 66–67 to help you answer the questions below:

4. Name two countries in Asia that border India.

5. Name two countries in Europe that border Spain.

6. Name two countries in Europe that border Greece.

7. Name the country in Africa that forms the southern boundary of Egypt.

Try It Yourself

Draw a map of your state. Leave room around the state to show the other states or countries that share borders with your state. If there are landscape features like rivers, lakes, or oceans on your state's borders, draw those, too. Label your state and the other states that surround it. Also label your state's capital. Use the United States political map on pages 70–71 to help you find your state and capital city.

Key Words: map scale

In England, if you took a trip from London to Liverpool, you would travel about 200 miles. But on a map, London and Liverpool may only be a few inches apart.

When you look at a map, how can you figure out the distance between two places? You can use the **map scale**. A map scale helps you figure out the real distance between two places. For example, the scale might show that one inch on the map equals 100 miles in the real world.

Find the scale in the lower left corner of this map. The abbreviation "mi" stands for miles, and "km" stands for kilometers. Miles and kilometers are two different units of measurement used to measure distance. One mile is longer than one kilometer. On this map, one inch equals 100 miles or 161 kilometers.

Here's an easy way to use the scale on this map:
- Take out a piece of paper or an index card.
- Put the paper right below the map scale. Copy the scale onto the paper. Make sure you mark the beginning and end of the scale. Your marks must be the same distance apart as the marks on the map scale.
- Write the same numbers on your paper as you see on the map scale.
- Your paper or index card is now your own map scale.

Now try using your scale. Find Cardiff and Reading on the map. Try to find the distance between Cardiff and Reading.

- Put your scale on the map so that the 0 mile mark is on Cardiff.

- Turn your paper so the 100 mile mark faces toward Reading.

- How many inches is it from Cardiff to Reading on this map?

- If one inch equals 100 miles on this map, how many miles is it from Cardiff to Reading?

That's right! It's about 100 miles from Cardiff to Reading.

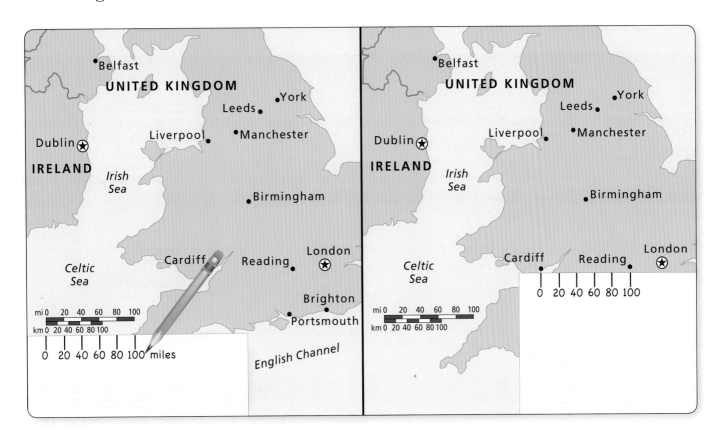

The distance from Cardiff to Reading was easy to measure. The distance between these cities on the map is one inch. Sometimes the distance on the map is not exactly an inch. When this happens, you have to estimate the distance.

Estimate the distances in miles between the cities listed below. **Use the map on page 30.**

1. Find the distance between Dublin and London.

2. Find the distance between Edinburgh and Manchester.

31

It's time for a trip to London! London is the capital of the United Kingdom. There's a lot to do in London. You can visit Buckingham Palace, where the Queen of England lives, or you might go for a nice boat ride on the Thames River. When you get hungry, have some fish and chips, or some tasty Indian food. Whatever you do, you'll want to use a map to find your way.

In London, the Houses of Parliament and the clock tower called Big Ben sit near the Thames River.

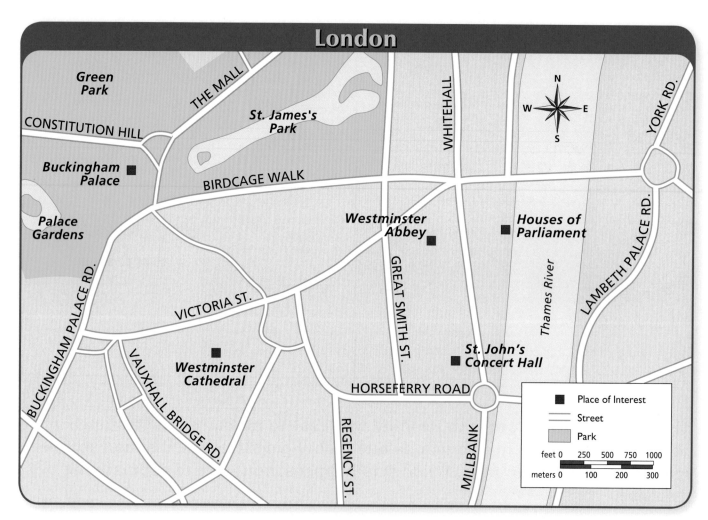

Different maps have different scales. Find the scale on this map. This scale looks different from the first one you saw. That's because this map shows London close-up. One inch on this map equals a much shorter distance than one inch on the map of the United Kingdom. On that map, one inch equaled 100 miles. On this map, one inch equals 1,000 feet, or 300 meters. (One meter is a little more than three feet.)

Buckingham Palace

The river called the Thames (say "temz")

Practice using the map scale to find distances on the map of London.

3. About how many feet is it from Westminster Abbey to the Houses of Parliament?

4. About how many meters is it from St. John's Concert Hall to Westminster Abbey?

5. If you walked from Buckingham Palace to the Thames River, about how many meters would you walk, 1,200 or 600?

6. About how many feet west of St. John's Concert Hall is Westminster Cathedral, 2,500 or 1,500?

Skill Builder

Review

1. If you were planning a trip, how could a map scale help you?

2. A map scale shows one inch equals 500 miles. Is this scale probably on a map of a city or a map of a continent? Why?

3. A map scale shows one inch equals 100 meters. Is this scale more likely to be on a map of a city or a map of a state? Why?

4. Which unit of measurement is longer, a mile or a kilometer?

5. Which unit of measurement is longer, a foot or a meter?

Try It Yourself

Look at the United States political map on pages 70–71. Find the map's scale. Use the scale to figure out how far it is from the city of Chicago, Illinois, to three other cities. Write these distances in miles and kilometers.

Key Words: landforms, coast, mountain, hill, valley, plain, plateau, island

"She'll be comin' round the mountain when she comes...."

"Down in the valley, the valley so low...."

Have you heard these old songs? Can you picture what a mountain and a valley look like? Mountains and valleys are **landforms**. Other landforms include hills, plateaus, plains, and islands. Look at the drawing below to see some common landforms.

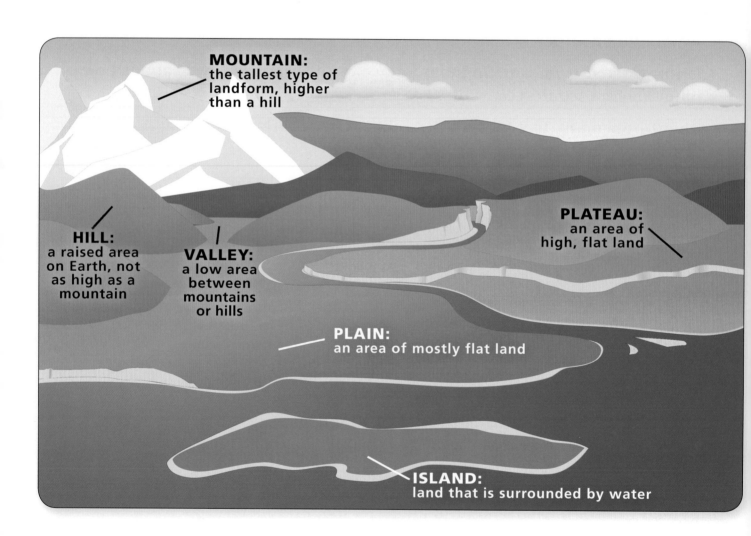

MOUNTAIN: the tallest type of landform, higher than a hill

HILL: a raised area on Earth, not as high as a mountain

VALLEY: a low area between mountains or hills

PLATEAU: an area of high, flat land

PLAIN: an area of mostly flat land

ISLAND: land that is surrounded by water

1. What is the difference between a hill and a mountain?

2. What is the difference between a plateau and a plain?

3. Would you see a valley in a place where the land is flat? Why or why not?

34

What landform am I?

Here are photographs of the same landforms that you see in the drawing on page 34. Look at the photographs and identify each landform.

4. mountains or hills?

5. valley or plateau?

6. plain or mountain?

7. plateau or mountain?

8. mountain or island?

9. plain or valley?

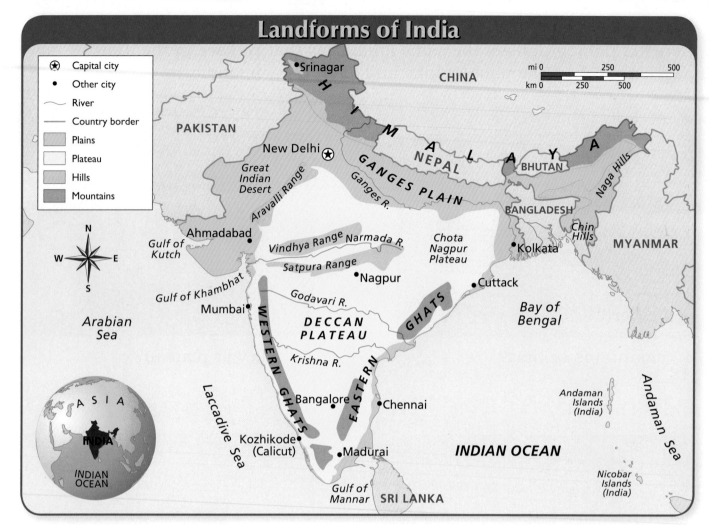

Landforms of India

Some maps show landforms. This is a map of India. India is a large country with many different landforms. The map shows some of India's mountains, including the Eastern Ghats and the Western Ghats. The highest mountains are called the Himalaya. The map also shows the Deccan Plateau and the Ganges Plain.

10. What color on the map shows mountains?

11. What color on the map shows plains?

12. Between which mountains is the Deccan Plateau located?

13. Find the Andaman and Nicobar Islands. Are these islands to the east or west of India?

14. Find the capital city, New Delhi. Is it in the mountains or plains?

15. Name one city on the Deccan Plateau.

16. What country borders India to the northwest?

17. Are India's highest mountains in the northern or southern part of the country?

36

Bodies of Water

The map of India also shows bodies of water. These include an ocean, seas, gulfs, a bay, and many rivers.

A river in India

- An ocean is a large body of salt water.
- A sea is a body of salt water that is smaller than an ocean.
- A gulf is a part of a sea or ocean that cuts into the land.
- A bay is a small body of water partly surrounded by land.
- A river is a body of fresh water that moves over land.

The place where land meets the ocean or the sea is called a **coast**. India's west coast is on the Arabian Sea. India's east coast is on the Bay of Bengal.

18. Find the Bay of Bengal. Name two countries on this bay.

19. Name the river that flows from the Himalaya to the Bay of Bengal.

20. Find the Arabian Sea. Name one country on this sea.

21. Name a gulf on India's west coast.

22. Name the ocean you see on this map.

Skill Builder

Review

1. Which is an area of flat high land, a valley or a plateau?
2. Which is a low area between mountains or hills, a plain or a valley?
3. Which is the taller landform, a plateau or a mountain?
4. Which is a large body of salt water, a sea or a river?
5. Which is bigger, a sea or an ocean?

Try It Yourself

Look at the United States physical map on pages 68–69. Find these landforms and bodies of water: the Rocky Mountains, the Great Plains, the Central Lowland, the Appalachian Mountains, the Gulf of Mexico, the Mississippi River, the Chesapeake Bay, and the Atlantic and Pacific Oceans.

Key Words: adapt, environment, desert, oasis, civilization

People must **adapt** to where they live. To adapt means to change or adjust your life to fit the world around you. If people live in a place that gets little rain, they must find ways to get water. If they live in a place that is very cold, they must find ways to keep warm.

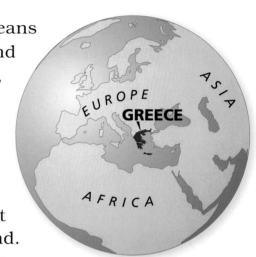

Long ago, the people of ancient Greece lived in rocky places like the one in the picture below. It is hard to grow crops for food on such rocky land. Also, in much of Greece, it does not rain often, so there is not enough water for most plants to grow well.

The people of ancient Greece found ways to adapt to this land. For example, they grew olive trees, which grow well in dry and rocky soil. They raised goats, which gave them meat and milk, as well as skins from which to make warm coats.

1. Do you think the houses in ancient Greece were made out of wood or stone? Why?

2. Give two reasons why it is hard to grow crops in Greece.

The rocky land of Greece

A branch on an olive tree in Greece

People have always adapted to different environments. An **environment** includes everything around you in a certain place—the land, the water, the air, the plants, and the animals. The environment affects the way people live, the houses they build, and the clothes they wear. Some people who live in the cold Andes mountains of South America raise llamas and alpacas. They use the wool of these animals to make warm clothing. That is one way they adapt to their cold environment.

A mountain peak in the Andes

Llama

People who live in the **desert** must adapt to an environment that gets very little rain. They must dig wells deep in the ground to find water. They also need to know where to find oases. An **oasis** is a place in the desert where there is water for plants to grow.

A desert dweller leading a camel

A tropical Island

High mountains

Look at these pictures. They show different environments. Think about how you would have to adapt to each environment. How would you change or adjust your life to live in each place?

A desert

39

In ancient times, people moved around from place to place hunting for food. When people learned how to farm and to raise their own animals for food, they no longer needed to move around. They began to settle down and live together in one area. This is how many of the first cities started.

The Yangtze River in China

Cities were the beginning of **civilizations**. To survive, people in early civilizations had to adapt to their environments. One thing they needed to survive was water. They used water for drinking and for growing plants. Their animals needed water to drink. It was easier to get water if they settled close to a river. The first civilizations began near big rivers. The map below shows the locations of some of these early civilizations that started near rivers.

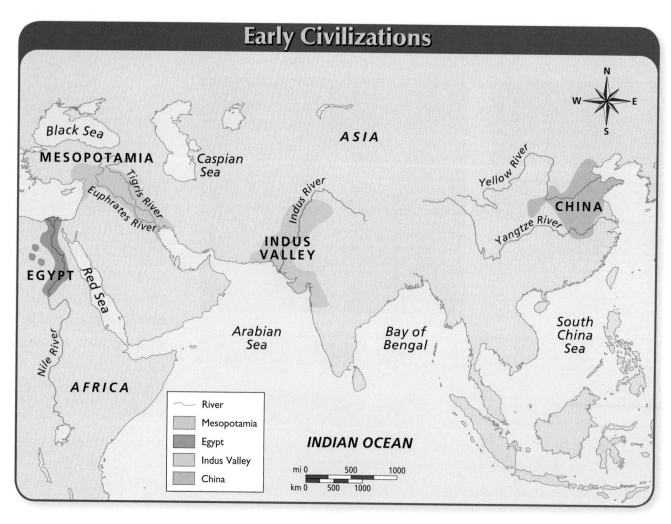

Early Civilizations

Black Sea

MESOPOTAMIA

Caspian Sea

ASIA

Tigris River

Euphrates River

Indus River

Yellow River

CHINA

Yangtze River

INDUS VALLEY

EGYPT

Red Sea

Nile River

Arabian Sea

Bay of Bengal

South China Sea

AFRICA

INDIAN OCEAN

River
Mesopotamia
Egypt
Indus Valley
China

mi 0   500   1000
km 0 500 1000

3. Find Egypt on the map on page 40. What river did the ancient Egyptians live around?

4. Find Mesopotamia. The name means "between rivers." Between what two rivers did this civilization grow?

5. Early civilization in China began near two big rivers. Look at the map. What are these two rivers?

6. What civilization began near the Indus River and Arabian Sea?

7. You have seen that many ancient civilizations started near big rivers. Rivers bring fresh water. Name three ways the people in these ancient civilizations used the water from the rivers.

The Indus River

Skill Builder

Review

1. True or False: A desert is an area that gets plenty of rain.

2. Why did early civilizations begin near large rivers?

3. Imagine you move to the high mountains. Describe one thing you would do to adapt to this environment.

4. Imagine you move to the desert. Describe one thing you would do to adapt to your new environment.

Try It Yourself

Look at the different environments in the pictures on page 39. In which environment would you most like to live? Imagine your life there. Explain why you decided to move there. Describe what you think would be the best and worst parts of living there.

Key Words: adapt, desert

Let's visit two very different countries, Austria and Egypt. Austria is in Europe. Egypt is in Africa.

Austria is farther north from the equator than Egypt. Places farther away from the equator are usually cooler. Austria's temperatures are usually not as warm as Egypt's.

In Austria, the winters are cold and it snows sometimes. People have to bundle up in thick, warm clothes. Austria's summers are warm, but not too hot.

In Egypt it gets very hot in the summer. In the winter, it sometimes gets cool, but not very cold. On winter nights, you might want a light jacket, but you would not need a heavy coat or mittens.

Austria gets some rain or snow all year round. The rain helps plants and trees grow. There are thick forests and green valleys. Many crops grow well in Austria because there is plenty of rainfall.

The Danube River in Austria

Egypt gets almost no rain at all. Egypt is in a desert. The driest places on Earth are called **deserts**. Few plants grow in such dry places. Much of Egypt is sandy without any grasses or trees. But trees do grow in Egypt along the big river called the Nile. The farms in Egypt are also near this river.

Austria has rolling hills and high mountains. Egypt is mostly flat. It has some mountains, but they are not as high as the mountains in Austria.

The Nile River in Egypt

Vienna and Cairo are both capital cities. Vienna is the capital of Austria. Cairo is the capital of Egypt. The people in Vienna and Cairo **adapt** to the changing weather and seasons in their cities.

One way that people in Vienna and Cairo adapt to where they live is in the different kinds of buildings they build. In Vienna, most of the buildings have slanted roofs. The slanted roofs let snow and rain slide off. The buildings in Austria are heated in the winter.

In Cairo, the buildings are very different. The roofs are not slanted. It never snows in Cairo, and it rarely rains, so the roofs can be flat. Long ago, people slept on their flat roofs to enjoy the cooler night air. Today, some new buildings in Cairo are air-conditioned.

Vienna, Austria

Cairo, Egypt

1. Which city gets more rain, Vienna or Cairo?

2. Which country is closer to the equator, Austria or Egypt?

3. Why do buildings in Vienna have slanted roofs?

4. In which country do people have to wear warmer clothes in the winter, Austria or Egypt?

5. Which country has a hotter summer, Austria or Egypt?

6. Which country has many rolling hills and tall mountains, Austria or Egypt?

7. Is the Nile River in Austria or Egypt?

Europe and Northern Africa

This map shows Austria and Egypt. Their capital cities, Vienna and Cairo, are about 1,500 miles apart.

8. On which continent is Austria located? On which continent is Egypt located?

9. Which country is farther north, Austria or Egypt?

10. Name two countries that border Austria.

11. Name two countries that border Egypt.

12. What direction would you travel if you went from Cairo to Vienna?

13. What is the name of the sea between Europe and Africa?

Where do I live?

For the questions below, think about what you have learned about Austria and Egypt.

a.

b.

14. Look at the pictures above. Which picture do you think was taken in Austria?

15. Which picture do you think was taken in Egypt?

16. My country is in the northern part of Africa and gets very little rain. Do I live in Austria or Egypt?

17. My city is on the Danube River. In the winter I have to wear a thick coat to protect me from the cold. Do I live in Vienna or Cairo?

Skill Builder

Review

1. On a world map or globe, locate Austria and Egypt. You can use the political world map on pages 66–67.

2. Describe one difference between Austria and Egypt.

3. Which city is in Europe, Vienna or Cairo?

4. Which country is in a desert, Austria or Egypt?

5. Which city is farther south, Vienna or Cairo?

Try It Yourself

Where do you live? Is the place where you live more like Austria or Egypt? Why?

Activity 11 Natural Resources

Key Words: natural resources, agriculture, mining, forestry

What did you have for dinner last night? Where did you sit when you ate? Do you know where your food and furniture come from? It did not just come from the supermarket or furniture store. There's more to the story than that!

Our food and furniture are made from **natural resources**. A natural resource is something we use that comes from nature. For example, forests are natural resources. We cut down trees to make lumber. Lumber is wood that has been cut from trees for people to use. We use lumber to build houses and make furniture.

We use some animals, such as cows and sheep, for food and clothing. These animals are natural resources. Plants like corn and wheat are also natural resources. Growing plants or raising animals is called **agriculture**.

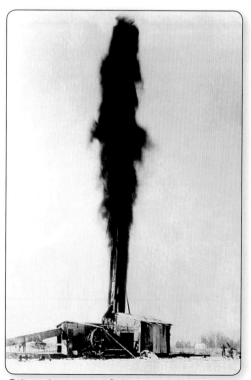

Oil gushing out of the ground

Look around you for something made of metal. You might see a pot made out of aluminum or a penny made of copper. Aluminum and copper are metals. Metals are also natural resources. Most metals come from underneath the ground. Mines are dug to bring metals out of the ground.

Look around the room you are in. How many lights are on? Is the heater or air conditioning on? All of these things use energy. In the United States, most of our energy comes from oil and coal. Oil and coal are both natural resources that come from under the ground.

You have learned about different kinds of natural resources:

- *animal resources*, such as cattle, chickens, or fish
- *plant resources*, such as trees, corn, or wheat
- *mineral resources*, such as copper or aluminum dug from mines in the ground
- *fossil fuels*, such as coal, oil, or natural gas, which are created over a very long time from the remains of plants and animals

a.

b.

c.

d.

1. Look at the pictures above. Identify the type of natural resources you see in each picture. Are they animal, plant, or mineral resources?

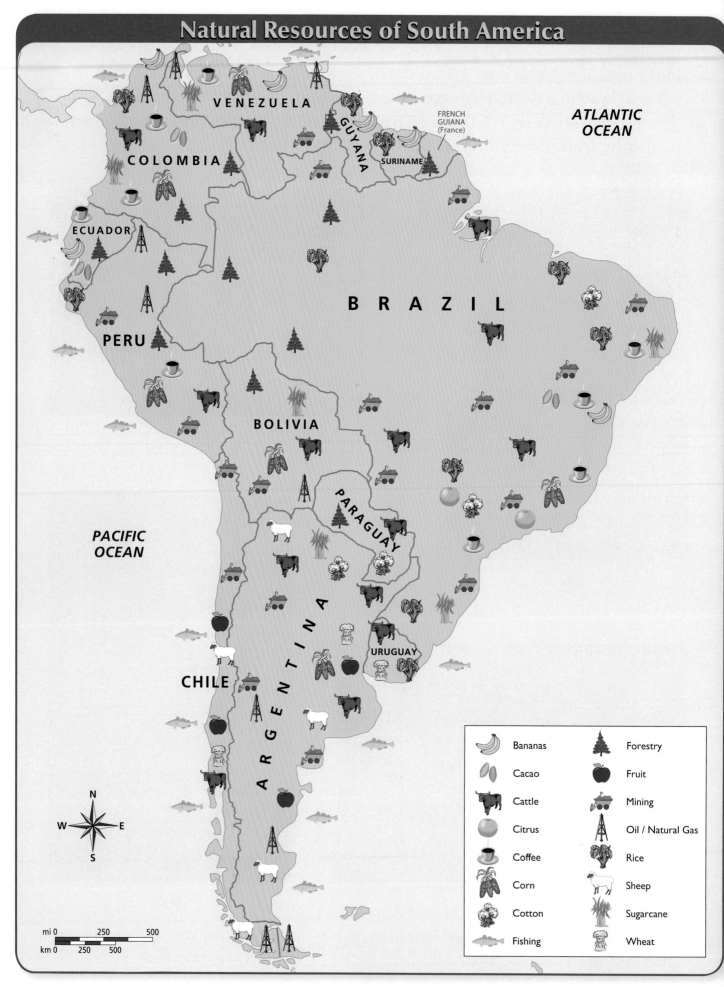

Oranges growing in South America

A farmer in South America

Some maps show natural resources. The map on page 48 shows some of the natural resources in South America. Look at the map key to identify the symbols for these resources. Look for these symbols on the map. For example, find the symbol for cacao on the key and then locate that symbol on the map. Cacao is a plant used to make chocolate. It grows in warm places near the equator. Other plants that grow in South America's warm areas are bananas and citrus fruits, such as oranges. The map also shows mining and forestry. **Mining** means taking mineral resources from the ground. **Forestry** means growing and taking care of trees, some of which will be cut down for lumber.

Look at the Natural Resources of South America map on page 48.

2. Name two animal resources in South America.

3. Name three plant resources in South America.

4. Which country is known for its sheep farming, Argentina or Venezuela?

5. Name three countries where coffee is grown.

6. In which country are fish a big resource, Paraguay or Peru?

7. In which country is citrus fruit grown, Brazil or Bolivia?

8. Name three natural resources found in Colombia.

9. Name three natural resources found in Brazil.

10. Name three natural resources found in Chile.

Natural Resources of Canada

Canada is the United States' neighbor to the north. Canada is divided into thirteen provinces and territories. Provinces and territories in Canada are similar to states in the United States.

Use the map key to find some of Canada's natural resources.

11. Name two animal resources in Canada.

12. Name two plant resources in Canada.

13. Which province has more mining, Ontario or Newfoundland?

14. Which province has more oil, Alberta or Québec?

15. Name two provinces or territories where fruit is grown.

16. Name two provinces or territories where fish are an important resource.

17. Name two provinces or territories where forestry is a big resource.

Will they last forever?

Some natural resources can last a long time if we take care of them. Animals have babies, and many plants grow back each year. If we are careful not to use too many animals, then we will have more. If we take care of the land, we can grow more trees and crops. We can renew animal and plant resources. But mineral resources do not grow. There is nothing we can do to renew them. If we use all of our oil and coal, there will be none left. We will have to get our energy from other sources, like the sun or the wind.

On a wind farm in California, wind turbines capture wind power to be changed into electricity.

Skill Builder

Review

1. Which is a mineral resource, lumber or copper?

2. Which is an example of agriculture, raising chickens or mining for gold?

3. Which resource would you find in South America but not in Canada, coffee or fish?

4. Which resource would you find in South America but not in Canada, lumber or cacao?

5. Which resource can be renewed, lumber or coal?

6. Which resource will run out and cannot be replaced, oil or fish?

Try It Yourself

List at least three natural resources you have used this week. Which type of resource is each: animal, plant, or mineral?

Graphs

Key Words: graph, picture graph, bar graph, circle graph

Imagine you take a walk in a park. You notice many kinds of trees. You decide to count how many of each kind of tree you see. For example, you count all the oak trees, all the maple trees, and all the willow trees. How can you quickly show the number of each kind of tree you have counted? One way is to make a **graph**.

Trees in a park

Picture Graphs

One type of graph is a **picture graph**, sometimes called a pictograph. Here is a picture graph of the trees in City Park.

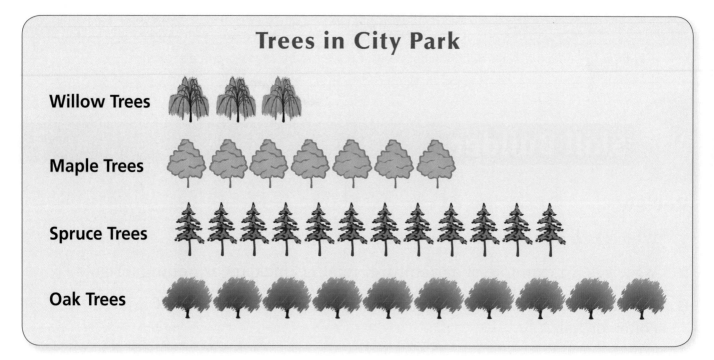

This graph uses pictures to show how many of each kind of tree is in the park. You see three pictures of a willow tree. This means that there are three willow trees in the park.

1. How many maple trees are in the park?
2. How many spruce trees are in the park?
3. How many oak trees are in the park?
4. List the types of trees in the park, from the most common to the least common.

Bar Graphs

Imagine that you are planning a trip to Rome, the capital city of Italy. You can go any time in the next year. When should you go? The weather in Rome can be rainy during some months. In other months, there is almost no rain at all. Would you like to go in the rainy months or the dry months?

Ruins of the Colosseum, an ancient stadium in Rome

The **bar graph** below shows you how much rain falls in Rome each month. A bar graph is a graph that uses bars to show how much or how many.

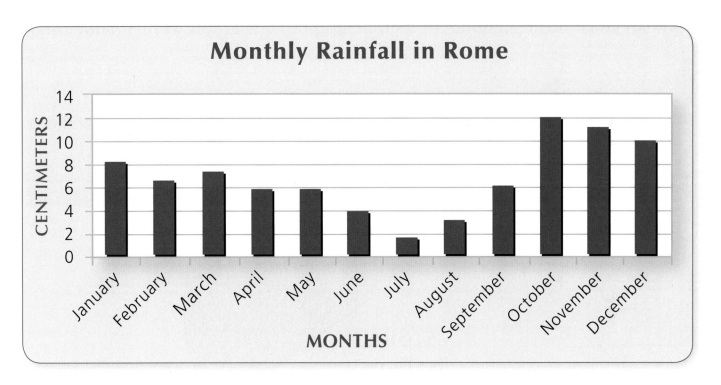

Look at the bottom line of the graph. It names the months. Each month has a bar. Now look at the numbers going up the left side of the graph. The numbers tell how many centimeters of rain fell. Each blue bar goes up as high as the number of centimeters of rain that fell in each month. The lines going across the graph help you find the number of centimeters on the left. There are about 2½ centimeters (cm) in an inch.

5. How many centimeters of rain fall in Rome in January?

6. How many centimeters of rain fall in Rome in September?

7. Which month gets the most rain?

8. Which month gets the least amount of rain?

53

Circle Graphs

Another kind of graph is a **circle graph**. Circle graphs are sometimes called pie charts because they look like pies. Circle graphs can show how a whole amount is divided into parts.

Imagine that you are visiting the town of Summerville. You want to see what the different houses on Elm Street are made of. You start at one end of Elm Street and walk all the way to the other end. You write down how many houses are brick, how many are stone, and how many are wood. This is what you find:

7 brick houses   **10 stone houses**   **3 wood houses**

You can show these amounts in a circle graph. Your graph will look like this:

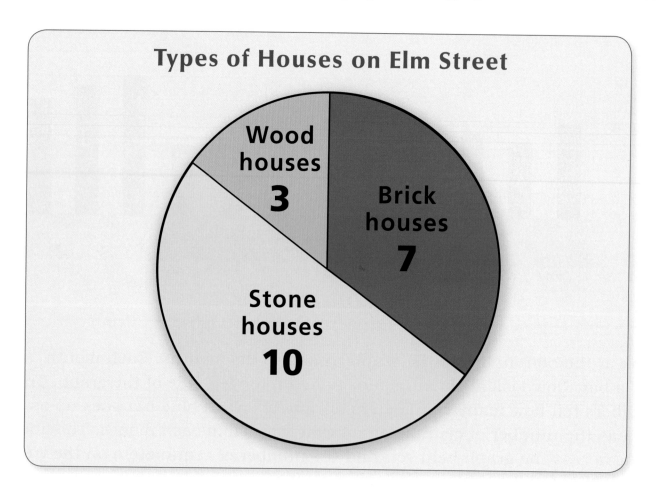

9. This circle graph looks like a pie that has been cut into three uneven pieces. Red stands for brick houses. What color stands for stone houses? What color stands for wood houses?

A circle graph lets you quickly compare how many. You can quickly see that most houses on Elm Street are made of stone. The numbers on this graph tell exactly how many houses of each kind there are on Elm Street.

Look at the graph and answer
these questions:

10. How many houses on Elm Street are
    made of brick?

11. How many houses on Elm Street are
    made of stone?

12. How many houses on Elm Street are
    made of wood?

13. What material was used least often to
    build the houses on Elm Street?

14. What material was used most often to
    build the houses on Elm Street?

15. How many houses of all kinds are there
    on Elm Street?

16. Could you show the same information
    about the houses on Elm Street in a
    bar graph? In a picture graph?

House made of wood

House made of brick

Skill Builder

Review

1. Name three different kinds of graphs.

2. What is another name for a circle graph?

3. Look at the circle graph on page 54. Imagine you show the same
   information in a bar graph. Which kind of house would have the tallest
   bar—brick, stone, or wood?

4. Give an example of things you could show in a bar graph.

5. Give an example of things you could show in a circle graph.

Try It Yourself

Look at the picture graph for trees in City Park. Use the same information to
make a bar graph. Write the numbers 2, 4, 6, 8, 10, and 12 going up the left
side of the bar graph. Draw a bar for each kind of tree. Each bar should go
up to the number of that kind of tree in City Park.

Activity 13 Time Lines

Key Words: time line

When you learn history, you hear a lot of dates and years. It can be hard to get them straight. It can also be hard to understand how long ago something happened.

Time Lines

A **time line** can help you learn and remember the order in which important events took place. Time lines are lines that have dates and events marked on them.

The Pilgrims arrive at Plymouth, Massachusetts.

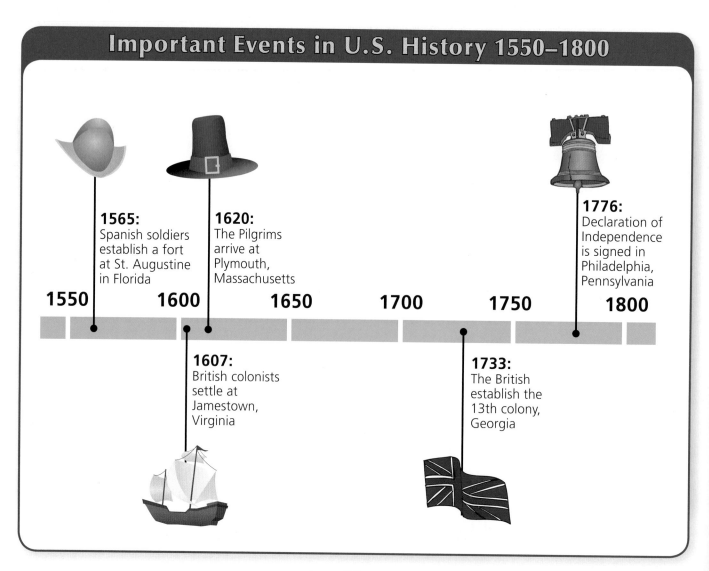

Important Events in U.S. History 1550–1800

1565:
Spanish soldiers establish a fort at St. Augustine in Florida

1620:
The Pilgrims arrive at Plymouth, Massachusetts

1776:
Declaration of Independence is signed in Philadelphia, Pennsylvania

1550 1600 1650 1700 1750 1800

1607:
British colonists settle at Jamestown, Virginia

1733:
The British establish the 13th colony, Georgia

56

The time line on page 56 shows five events in United States history. These events happened in 1565, 1607, 1620, 1733, and 1776. The time line shows years beginning with 1550 and ending at 1800. Each small break in the line marks 50 years. The years are labeled so they are easy to see.

Signing of the Declaration of Independence, 1776

George Washington

Each historical event is marked on the time line. The earliest event, which took place in 1565, is the farthest to the left. When you move to the right on the time line, you move forward in time. The year 1607 came after 1565. The year 1620 came even later. The last event marked on this time line took place in 1776.

Study the time line on page 56 and answer the questions below.

1. Which event on the time line happened first?

2. Which event on the time line happened last?

3. Which two events happened close together in time?

4. In what year did the Pilgrims arrive in Plymouth, Massachusetts?

5. In what year did the British colonists settle at Jamestown, Virginia?

6. George Washington was the first president of the United States. He was born in 1732. The year 1732 is not marked on the time line. Put your finger on the time line to show where the year 1732 should be marked.

7. How many years are shown on the time line? You can figure this out by subtracting 1550 from 1800. You may want to ask an adult for help.

Important Events in U.S. History 1775–1785

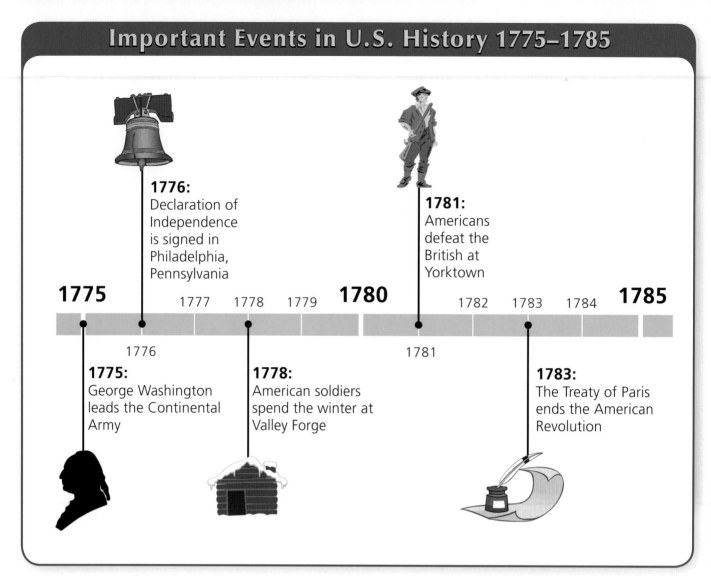

Some time lines show long periods of time. Others show shorter periods of time.

8. How many years are shown on the time line above?

9. In what year did the Americans defeat the British at Yorktown?

10. In what year did George Washington lead the Continental Army?

11. Which event happened first, the winter at Valley Forge or the battle at Yorktown?

12. Which event happened first, the Treaty of Paris or the signing of the Declaration of Independence?

13. Which event happened two years after the signing of the Declaration of Independence?

14. What happened three years before the winter at Valley Forge?

You've looked at time lines with the dates of some important events in United States history. Imagine you want to visit some of the places where those events took place. Find the places on the map.

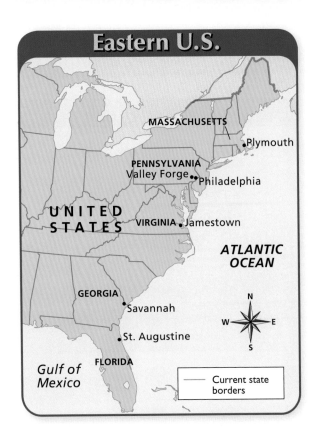

Eastern U.S.

15. The last British colony was settled in Savannah. In which state is Savannah located?

16. In which state was Jamestown settled?

17. In which city in Pennsylvania was the Declaration of Independence signed?

18. American soldiers spent the winter in Valley Forge in 1781. In which state is Valley Forge located?

19. Where did the Pilgrims land in 1620?

20. What city did Spanish soldiers establish as a fort in 1565?

Skill Builder

Review

1. How can time lines help you learn about history?

2. Time lines don't have to be about famous historical events. What else can you show on a time line? Try to think of at least one example.

Try It Yourself

Make a time line about a week in your life. Follow these steps:

a. Turn a piece of paper sideways. Use a ruler to draw a straight line across the paper.

b. Make a small mark on the left end of the time line. Under this mark, write Monday.

c. Use the ruler to measure one inch to the right of Monday. Make another mark here. Label this mark Tuesday.

d. Use the ruler again to measure one inch to the right of Tuesday. Keep doing this until you have written all the days of the week.

e. Think of one thing that happened each day. Under each day, write what happened. If you want to, you can draw pictures, too.

Map Review

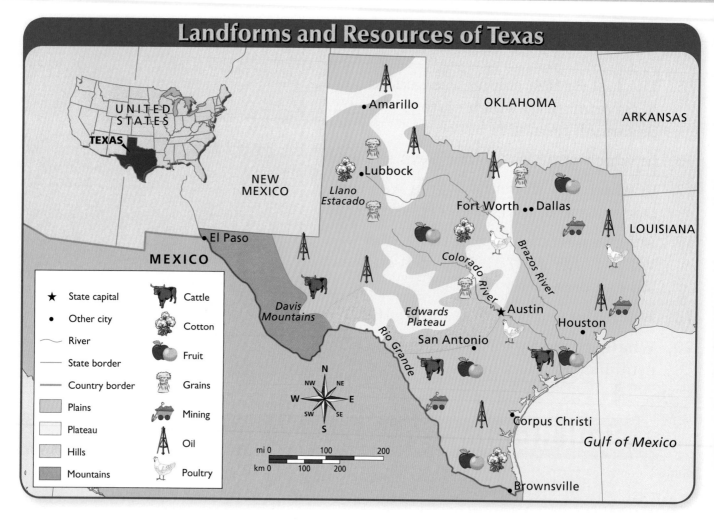

Landforms and Resources of Texas

Look at the map of Texas and answer the following questions.

1. Which city is the state capital of Texas?

2. Name four states that share a border with Texas.

3. Which country shares a border with Texas?

4. What body of water touches Louisiana, Texas, and Mexico?

5. Which color on the map shows an area of mountains?

6. Name two animal resources found in Texas.

7. Is the city of Houston on the plains or in the mountains?

8. What is the name of the large plateau in Texas?

9. On what type of land in Texas can you grow fruit and raise cattle?

10. Which river runs through the capital city of Texas?

11. The river called the Río Grande flows into the Gulf of Mexico. Which direction does it flow, southwest or southeast?

12. In which part of the United States is Texas located, north or south?

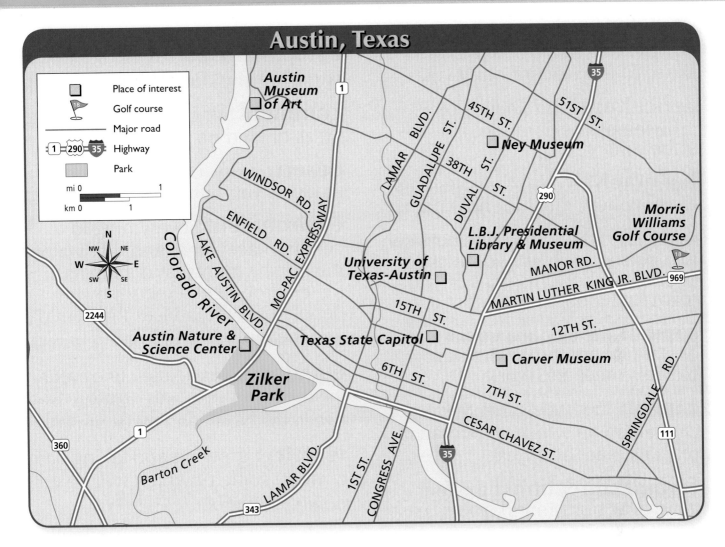

Austin, Texas

Legend:
- Place of interest
- Golf course
- Major road
- Highway (1, 290, 35)
- Park
- mi 0 — 1
- km 0 — 1

Austin Museum of Art

Ney Museum

45TH ST.

51ST ST.

LAMAR BLVD.

GUADALUPE ST.

38TH ST.

DUVAL ST.

290

Morris Williams Golf Course

WINDSOR RD.

ENFIELD RD.

L.B.J. Presidential Library & Museum

University of Texas-Austin

MANOR RD.

MARTIN LUTHER KING JR. BLVD.

969

Colorado River

LAKE AUSTIN BLVD.

MO-PAC EXPRESSWAY

15TH ST.

2244

Austin Nature & Science Center

Texas State Capitol

12TH ST.

Carver Museum

SPRINGDALE RD.

Zilker Park

6TH ST.

7TH ST.

1

360

CESAR CHAVEZ ST.

111

Barton Creek

LAMAR BLVD.

1ST ST.

CONGRESS AVE.

35

343

Look at the map of the city of Austin and answer the following questions.

13. What is the name of the park located beside the Colorado River?

14. Which two places of interest are located near the Colorado River?

15. Which road is located closest to the Carver Museum?

16. What direction would you travel to get from the Austin Nature & Science Center to the Texas State Capitol?

17. Which important place of interest is located near the corner of 15th Street and 1st Street?

18. Name the number of at least one highway that runs through Austin.

19. What is the distance in miles between the Texas State Capitol and the L.B.J. Presidential Library?

20. Which of these places of interest is located farther north on the map—the Carver Museum or the Austin Museum of Art?

Glossary

adapt: to change or adjust your life to fit the world around you

agriculture: the science of growing plants or raising animals to be sold

bar graph: a chart that uses bars to show how much or how many

border: the dividing line between two places, such as two states or countries, shown as lines on most maps and globes

capital: the city in a country or state where the government officials meet and work

capitol: the building in the capital city in which government officials meet and work

cardinal directions: the four main directions (north, south, east and west)

circle graph: a circle shaped drawing, also called a pie chart, that shows how a whole amount is divided into parts

civilization: a highly developed and organized group of people, often living in cities, marked by achievements in writing, art, and technology

coast: the land next to the ocean or sea; the seashore

community: a group of people who live and work in the same area and who have something in common with each other

compass rose: a symbol showing the directions on a map

continent: one of the seven large areas of land on Earth

desert: a dry, often sandy area that gets very little rain

environment: everything in a certain place—the land, the water, the air, the plants, and animals; the environment affects the way people live, the houses they build, and the clothes they wear

equator: an imaginary line around the middle of the Earth, halfway between the North and the South Poles

forestry: growing and taking care of trees, some of which will be cut down for lumber

globe: a ball-shaped model of the Earth

graph: a type of drawing used to show how much or how many, or to compare amounts of different things

hemisphere: one half of the Earth; the Earth can be divided into four hemispheres (Eastern, Western, Northern, and Southern)

hill: a raised area on Earth, not as high as a mountain

intermediate directions: the directions in between the cardinal directions (northwest, northeast, southwest, and southeast)

island: land that is completely surrounded by water

landforms: physical features on the Earth such as mountains, hills, or islands

locator map: a map, often placed within a larger map, that shows the location of a place in a city, state, country, or the world

map: a detailed drawing of an area, often showing features such as towns and roads or rivers and mountains

map key: a guide to what the symbols on a map mean

map scale: a measurement guide on a map that helps you figure out the real distances between places

mining: digging into the Earth to remove mineral resources such as coal

mountain: the tallest type of landform, higher than a hill

natural resources: materials we use that come from nature, such as wood from forests, water from rivers, or coal from the ground

neighborhood: a small area or section of a city or town where people live together

North Pole: the point on Earth that is as far north as you can go

oasis: a place in the desert where there is water for plants to grow

ocean: a large body of salt water on the Earth's surface

picture graph: a kind of drawing, also called a pictograph, that uses pictures to show how much or how many

plain: an area of mostly flat land

plateau: an area of high, flat land

political map: a map that shows the locations of countries and the borders between them, and often the locations of states and cities

prime meridian: an imaginary line going around the Earth and running through the North and South Poles

satellite image: a picture sent to Earth taken from a spacecraft

South Pole: the point on Earth that is as far south as you can go

time line: a line showing dates and events in the order that they happened

valley: a low area between mountains or hills

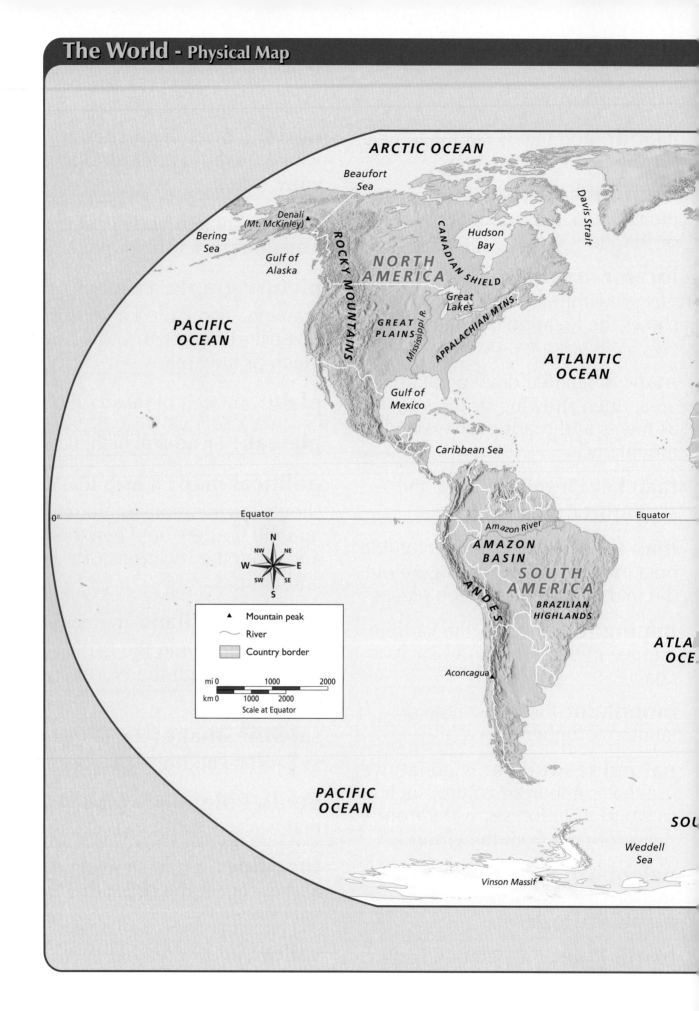

ARCTIC OCEAN

Beaufort
Sea

Davis Strait

Denali ▲
(Mt. McKinley)

Bering
Sea

Gulf of
Alaska

ROCKY MOUNTAINS

CANADIAN SHIELD

Hudson
Bay

NORTH
AMERICA

Great
Lakes

APPALACHIAN MTNS.

GREAT
PLAINS

Mississippi R.

PACIFIC
OCEAN

ATLANTIC
OCEAN

Gulf of
Mexico

Caribbean Sea

Equator   Equator

Amazon River

AMAZON
BASIN

SOUTH
AMERICA

ANDES

BRAZILIAN
HIGHLANDS

ATLA
OCE

	N	
NW		NE
W		E
SW		SE
	S	

▲	Mountain peak
⌒	River
▨	Country border

Aconcagua ▲

mi 0   1000   2000
km 0   1000   2000
Scale at Equator

PACIFIC
OCEAN

SOU

Weddell
Sea

Vinson Massif ▲

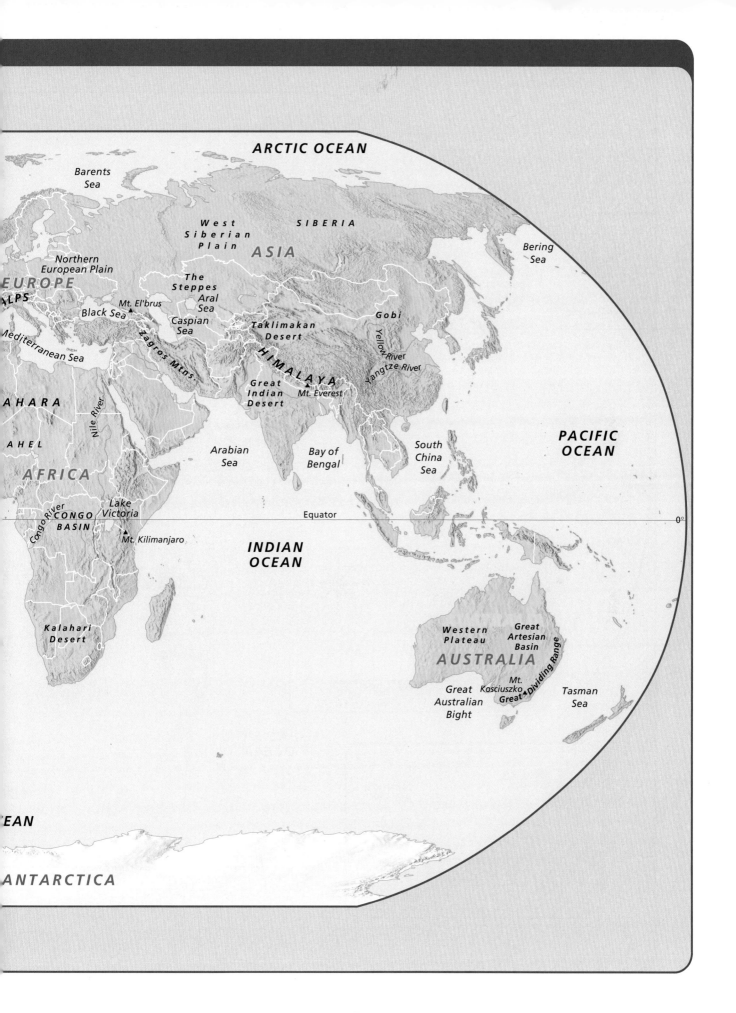

ARCTIC OCEAN

Barents
Sea

West
Siberian
Plain

SIBERIA

ASIA

Bering
Sea

Northern
European Plain

The
Steppes
Aral
Sea

EUROPE

ALPS

Mt. El'brus

Black Sea

Caspian
Sea

Taklimakan
Desert

Gobi

Yellow
River

Zagros Mtns.

Mediterranean Sea

HIMALAYA

Yangtze River

SAHARA

Nile River

Great
Indian
Desert

Mt. Everest

PACIFIC
OCEAN

SAHEL

Arabian
Sea

Bay of
Bengal

South
China
Sea

AFRICA

Congo River

CONGO
BASIN

Lake
Victoria

Equator

0°

Mt. Kilimanjaro

INDIAN
OCEAN

Kalahari
Desert

Western
Plateau

Great
Artesian
Basin

AUSTRALIA

Great
Dividing Range

Great
Australian
Bight

Mt.
Kosciuszko

Tasman
Sea

Great

OCEAN

ANTARCTICA

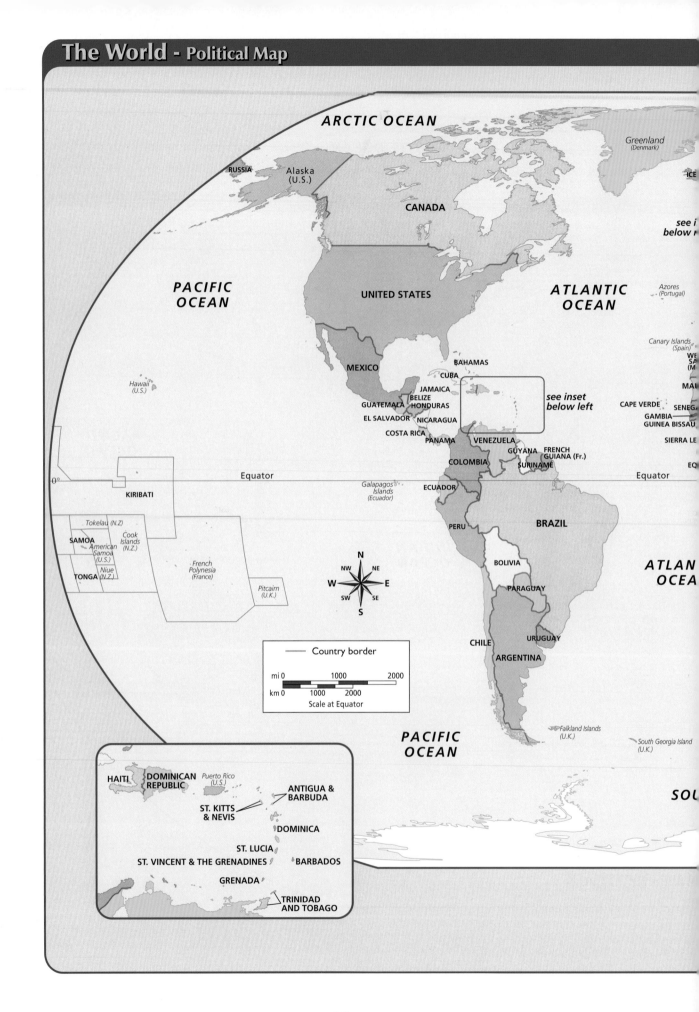

ARCTIC OCEAN

Greenland
(Denmark)

RUSSIA

Alaska
(U.S.)

ICE

CANADA

see i
below r

PACIFIC
OCEAN

UNITED STATES

ATLANTIC
OCEAN

Azores
(Portugal)

Canary Islands
(Spain)

WE
SA
(M

MEXICO

BAHAMAS

CUBA

JAMAICA

BELIZE

HONDURAS

GUATEMALA

EL SALVADOR

NICARAGUA

COSTA RICA

PANAMA

see inset
below left

CAPE VERDE

GAMBIA

GUINEA BISSAU

MAL

SENEGA

SIERRA LE

Hawaii
(U.S.)

VENEZUELA

GUYANA

FRENCH
GUIANA (Fr.)

SURINAME

COLOMBIA

EQ

Equator

Galapagos
Islands
(Ecuador)

ECUADOR

Equator

0°

KIRIBATI

PERU

BRAZIL

Tokelau (N.Z)

SAMOA

American
Samoa
(U.S.)

Cook
Islands
(N.Z.)

BOLIVIA

ATLAN
OCEA

TONGA

Niue
(N.Z.)

French
Polynesia
(France)

PARAGUAY

Pitcairn
(U.K.)

N

NW   NE

W   E

SW   SE

S

CHILE

URUGUAY

ARGENTINA

Country border

mi 0   1000   2000

km 0   1000   2000

Scale at Equator

PACIFIC
OCEAN

Falkland Islands
(U.K.)

South Georgia Island
(U.K.)

SOU

HAITI

DOMINICAN
REPUBLIC

Puerto Rico
(U.S.)

ANTIGUA &
BARBUDA

ST. KITTS
& NEVIS

DOMINICA

ST. LUCIA

ST. VINCENT & THE GRENADINES

BARBADOS

GRENADA

TRINIDAD
AND TOBAGO

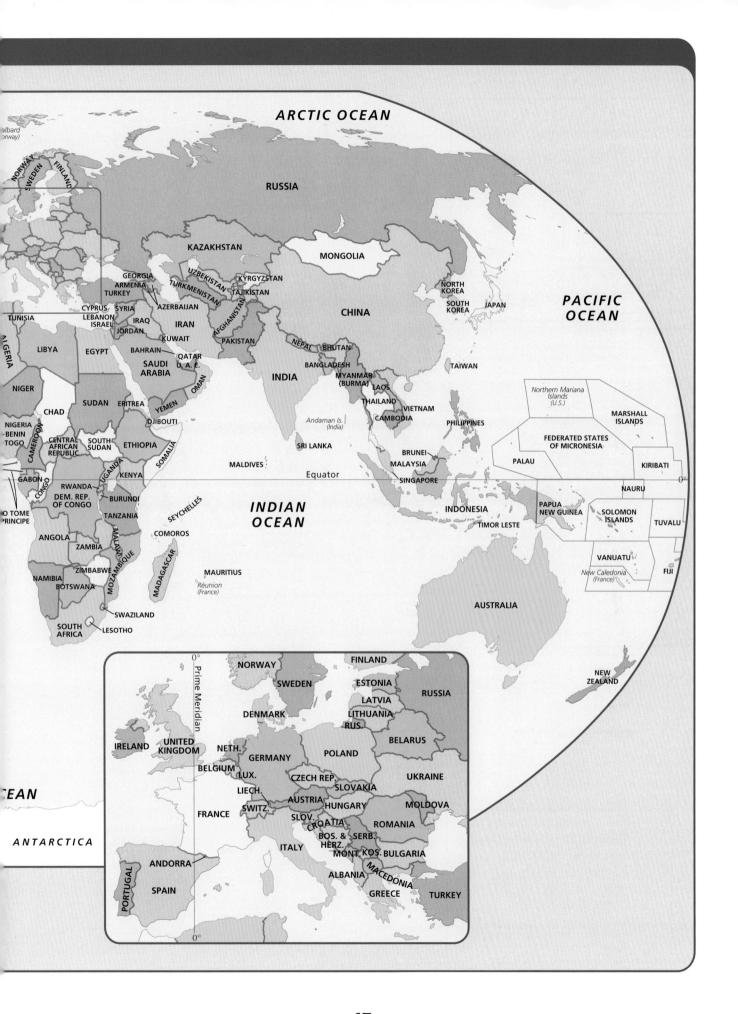

ARCTIC OCEAN

RUSSIA

Svalbard
(Norway)

NORWAY
SWEDEN
FINLAND

KAZAKHSTAN
MONGOLIA

GEORGIA
ARMENIA
TURKEY
CYPRUS SYRIA
LEBANON
ISRAEL
TUNISIA
JORDAN
ALGERIA
LIBYA
EGYPT

UZBEKISTAN
KYRGYZSTAN
TURKMENISTAN
TAJIKISTAN
AZERBAIJAN
IRAQ
IRAN
KUWAIT
AFGHANISTAN
BAHRAIN
QATAR
U.A.E.
PAKISTAN

NORTH
KOREA
SOUTH
KOREA
JAPAN

CHINA

PACIFIC
OCEAN

NIGER
CHAD
SUDAN
ERITREA
YEMEN
DJIBOUTI

SAUDI
ARABIA

OMAN

NEPAL BHUTAN
BANGLADESH
INDIA
MYANMAR
(BURMA)
LAOS
TAIWAN

Northern Mariana
Islands
(U.S.)

MARSHALL
ISLANDS

NIGERIA
BENIN
TOGO
CAMEROON
CENTRAL
AFRICAN
REPUBLIC
SOUTH
SUDAN
ETHIOPIA
SOMALIA

THAILAND
CAMBODIA
VIETNAM

Andaman Is.
(India)

SRI LANKA

PHILIPPINES

FEDERATED STATES
OF MICRONESIA

PALAU
KIRIBATI

GABON
CONGO
UGANDA
KENYA
RWANDA
BURUNDI
DEM. REP.
OF CONGO
SAO TOME
PRINCIPE
TANZANIA
SEYCHELLES
COMOROS

MALDIVES
Equator

BRUNEI
MALAYSIA
SINGAPORE

NAURU
0°

INDIAN
OCEAN

INDONESIA
PAPUA
NEW GUINEA
SOLOMON
ISLANDS
TUVALU

TIMOR LESTE

ANGOLA
ZAMBIA
MALAWI
MOZAMBIQUE
MADAGASCAR
ZIMBABWE
NAMIBIA
BOTSWANA
MAURITIUS
Réunion
(France)

VANUATU
New Caledonia
(France)
FIJI

SWAZILAND
SOUTH
AFRICA
LESOTHO

AUSTRALIA

NEW
ZEALAND

OCEAN

ANTARCTICA

Europe inset

0°
Prime Meridian

NORWAY
FINLAND
SWEDEN
ESTONIA
DENMARK
LATVIA
LITHUANIA
RUS.
RUSSIA

IRELAND
UNITED
KINGDOM
NETH.
BELGIUM
LUX.
GERMANY
POLAND
BELARUS

LIECH.
CZECH REP.
SLOVAKIA
UKRAINE

FRANCE
SWITZ.
AUSTRIA
HUNGARY
SLOV.
CROATIA
BOS. &
HERZ.
SERB.
ROMANIA
MOLDOVA

ITALY
MONT. KOS. BULGARIA
ANDORRA
ALBANIA
MACEDONIA

PORTUGAL
SPAIN
GREECE
TURKEY

0°

67

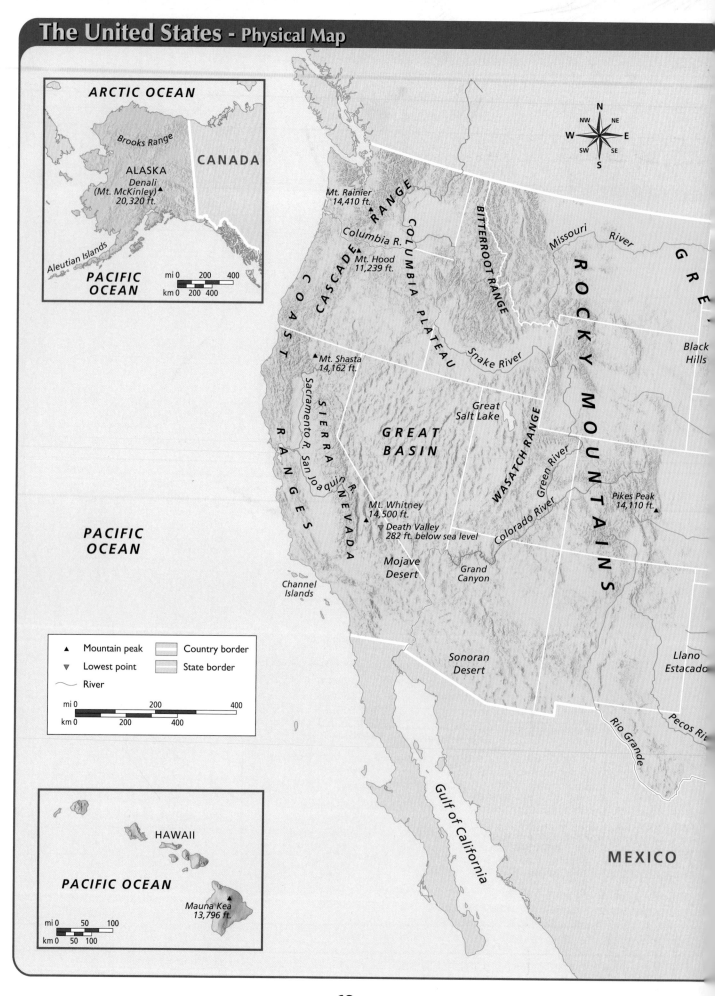

ARCTIC OCEAN

Brooks Range

ALASKA
Denali
(Mt. McKinley) ▲
20,320 ft.

CANADA

Aleutian Islands

PACIFIC
OCEAN

mi 0   200   400
km 0   200   400

N
NW   NE
W ✦ E
SW   SE
S

Mt. Rainier
14,410 ft.

COAST RANGE

CASCADE RANGE

Columbia R.

COLUMBIA PLATEAU

Mt. Hood ▲
11,239 ft.

BITTERROOT RANGE

Missouri   River

ROCKY MOUNTAINS

GRE

Black
Hills

Mt. Shasta ▲
14,162 ft.

Snake River

SIERRA NEVADA

Sacramento R.

San Joaquin R.

Great
Salt Lake

GREAT
BASIN

WASATCH RANGE

Green River

PACIFIC
OCEAN

Mt. Whitney ▲
14,500 ft.

Death Valley ▽
282 ft. below sea level

Colorado River

Pikes Peak
14,110 ft. ▲

Mojave
Desert

Grand
Canyon

Channel
Islands

Llano
Estacado

Sonoran
Desert

▲ Mountain peak   Country border
▽ Lowest point   State border
〜 River

mi 0   200   400
km 0   200   400

Rio Grande

Pecos Riv

Gulf of California

MEXICO

HAWAII

PACIFIC OCEAN

Mauna Kea
13,796 ft. ▲

mi 0   50   100
km 0   50   100

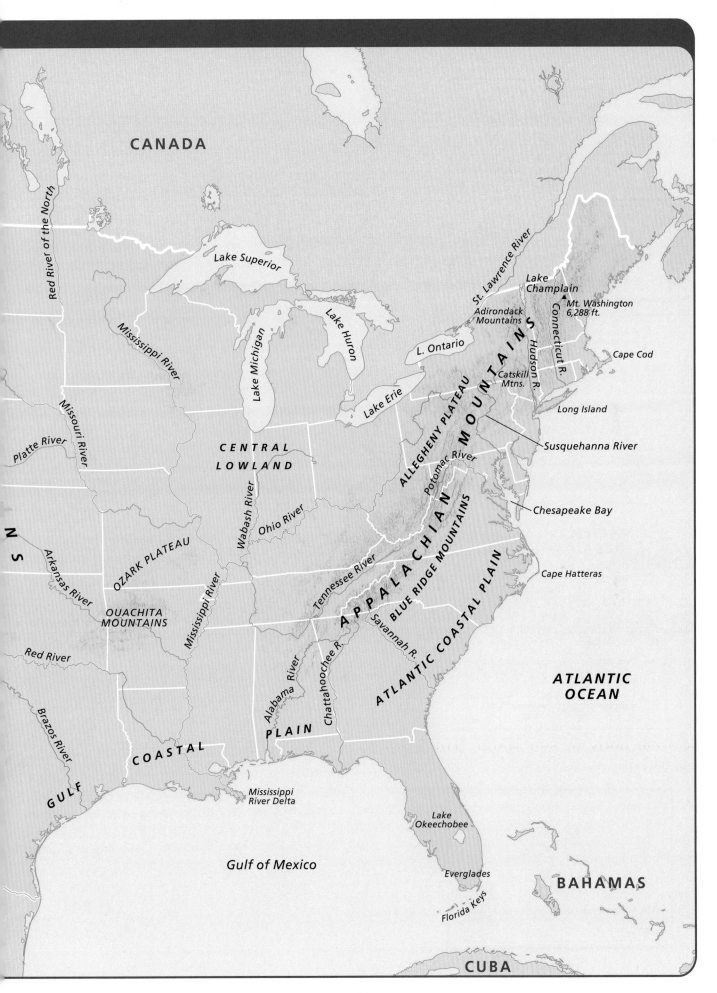

CANADA

Red River of the North

Lake Superior

St. Lawrence River

Lake Champlain

Mississippi River

Lake Michigan

Lake Huron

Adirondack Mountains

Mt. Washington 6,288 ft.

Connecticut R.

Missouri River

L. Ontario

Cape Cod

Platte River

Lake Erie

ALLEGHENY PLATEAU

Catskill Mtns.

Hudson R.

Long Island

Susquehanna River

CENTRAL LOWLAND

Potomac River

Chesapeake Bay

Wabash River

Ohio River

MOUNTAINS

NS

Arkansas River

OZARK PLATEAU

Mississippi River

Tennessee River

APPALACHIAN

BLUE RIDGE MOUNTAINS

Cape Hatteras

OUACHITA MOUNTAINS

Red River

Alabama River

Chattahoochee R.

Savannah R.

ATLANTIC COASTAL PLAIN

ATLANTIC OCEAN

Brazos River

COASTAL

PLAIN

GULF

Mississippi River Delta

Lake Okeechobee

Gulf of Mexico

Everglades

BAHAMAS

Florida Keys

CUBA

69

The United States - Political Map

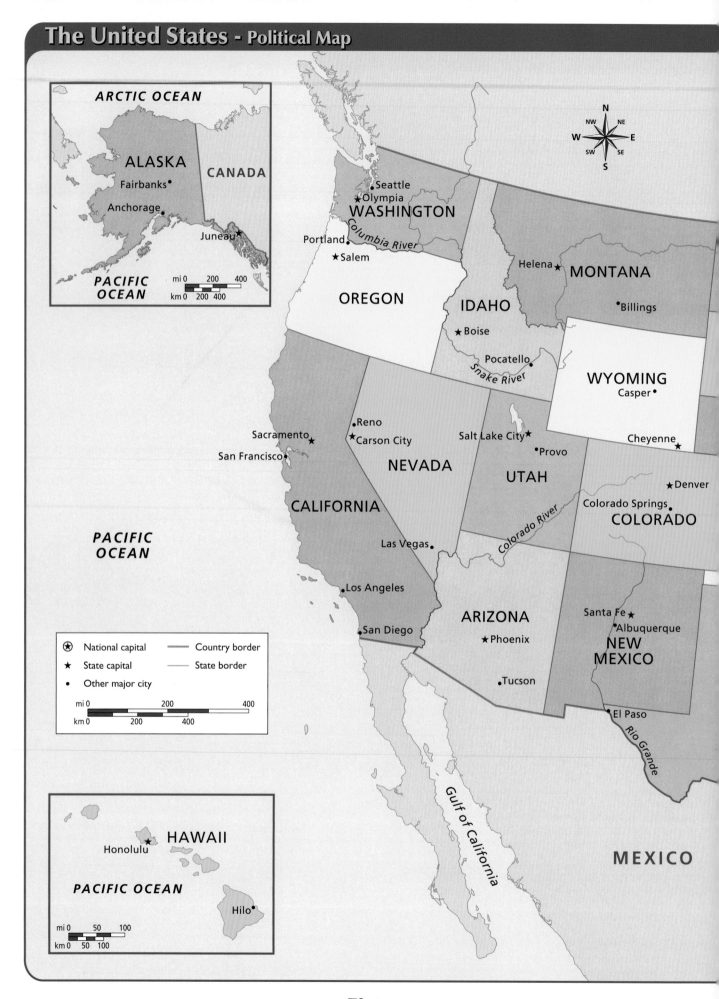

ARCTIC OCEAN

ALASKA

CANADA

Fairbanks•

•Anchorage

Juneau★

PACIFIC OCEAN

mi 0   200   400
km 0   200   400

•Seattle
★Olympia
WASHINGTON

Portland•
Columbia River
★Salem

OREGON

Helena ★   MONTANA

IDAHO
★Boise
•Billings

Pocatello•
Snake River

WYOMING
Casper •

•Reno
★Carson City

Salt Lake City ★

Cheyenne
★

Sacramento ★

•Provo

★Denver

San Francisco•

NEVADA

UTAH

Colorado Springs •

COLORADO

CALIFORNIA

Colorado River

PACIFIC OCEAN

Las Vegas•

•Los Angeles

San Diego•

ARIZONA
★Phoenix

Santa Fe ★
•Albuquerque

NEW MEXICO

•Tucson

El Paso•

Rio Grande

National capital
State capital
Other major city
Country border
State border

mi 0   200   400
km 0   200   400

Gulf of California

HAWAII
Honolulu ★

•Hilo

PACIFIC OCEAN

mi 0   50   100
km 0   50   100

MEXICO

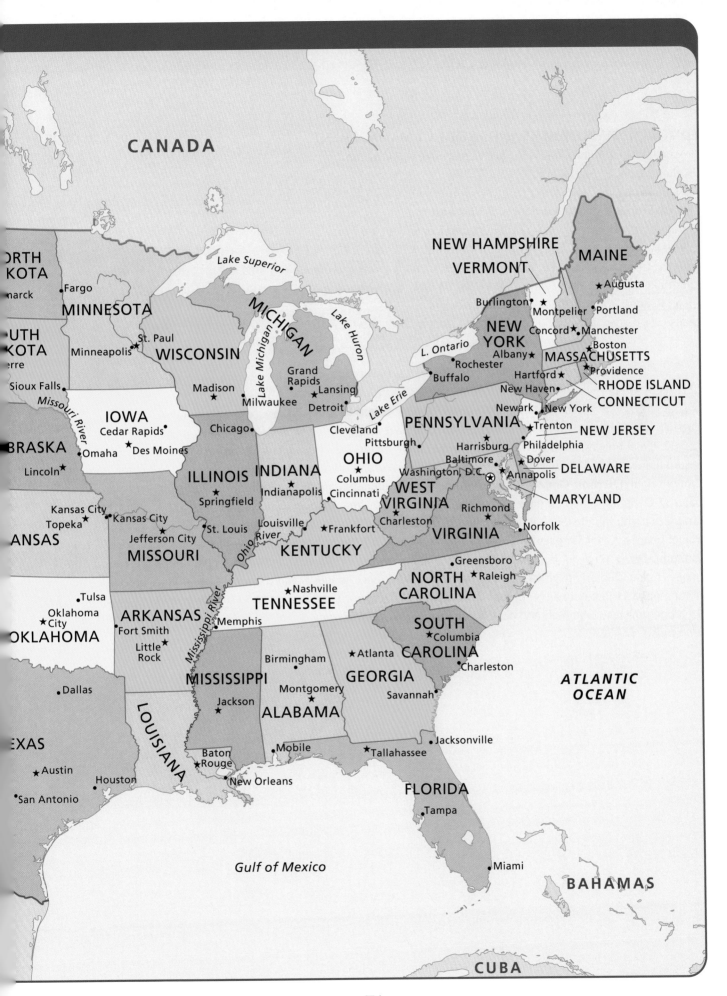

CANADA

Lake Superior

ORTH
KOTA
•marck ★Fargo
MINNESOTA

UTH
KOTA
erre
★Sioux Falls
Minneapolis •St. Paul ★
WISCONSIN

Lake Michigan

MICHIGAN
Grand
Rapids•
Madison ★ •Lansing
Milwaukee Detroit•

Lake Huron

Missouri River
IOWA
Cedar Rapids•
BRASKA
Omaha• •Des Moines ★
Lincoln•★

Chicago•
ILLINOIS INDIANA
Springfield★ Indianapolis★

Cleveland•
OHIO
Columbus★
Cincinnati•

Lake Erie

L. Ontario
Rochester•
Buffalo•

NEW HAMPSHIRE
VERMONT
Burlington• Montpelier•
NEW
YORK
Albany★

MAINE
★Augusta
•Portland
Concord★ •Manchester
Boston•
MASSACHUSETTS
Hartford★ Providence•
•New Haven
RHODE ISLAND
CONNECTICUT
Newark• •New York

PENNSYLVANIA
Pittsburgh•
Harrisburg★
Baltimore•
Washington, D.C.⊛ Annapolis★
WEST
VIRGINIA
Charleston★

Trenton★
Philadelphia•
NEW JERSEY
•Dover
DELAWARE

MARYLAND

KANSAS
ANSAS
Kansas City•
Topeka•★ ★Kansas City
Jefferson City★
MISSOURI
St. Louis•
Louisville•
Ohio River
Frankfort•★
KENTUCKY

Richmond★
Norfolk•
VIRGINIA

Greensboro•
★Raleigh
NORTH
CAROLINA

OKLAHOMA
•Tulsa
Oklahoma
★City
OKLAHOMA
ARKANSAS
Fort Smith•
Little ★
Rock

Mississippi River
★Nashville
TENNESSEE
Memphis•

Birmingham•

SOUTH
•Columbia
CAROLINA
★Atlanta
•Charleston

EXAS
•Dallas
★Austin
Houston•
•San Antonio
LOUISIANA
MISSISSIPPI
Jackson★
Montgomery
★
ALABAMA
Mobile•
GEORGIA
•Savannah

•Jacksonville
★Tallahassee

ATLANTIC
OCEAN

Baton
Rouge★
•New Orleans

FLORIDA
•Tampa

Gulf of Mexico

•Miami

BAHAMAS

CUBA

71

Credits

EDITORIAL DEVELOPMENT AND PRODUCT MANAGEMENT
Product Development: *Charles Regan, Vice President, Maps.com*
Product Manager: *Martin Walz*
Content Writer: *Betsy Hedberg*
Design, Production, and Illustration: *Bill Hansen*
Editor: *John Holdren, Director of Content and Curriculum, K12 Inc.*
Editor: *Patricia Pearson, History Content Specialist, K12 Inc.*
Editorial Consultant: *John G. Agnone, Director of Publications and Media, K12 Inc.*
Editorial Consultant: *Luke Ohrn*
Clean Reader: *Bud Knecht, Senior Editor, K12 Inc.*
Maps: *Maps.com (Martha Bostwick - Lead Cartographer), Martin Walz*

PHOTGRAPHS
page 6 NASA / Reto Stöckl / NASA-GRC; **page 7** NASA; **page 11** Jupiter images / Brand X Pictures / *Steven Allen*; **page 12** Freeze Frame Studio, Inc./iStockphoto.com; **page 16** Jupiter images / Liquid library; **page 20** NASA; **page 27** Lonely Planet Images, *Greg Gawlowski*; **page 32** Jupiter images / Brand X Pictures / *Steven Allen*; **page 33** Jupiter images / Liquid library; **page 35** Lonely Planet Images, *Richard I'Anson* (top right); Jupiter images / Brand X Pictures / *Steven Allen* (bottom right) Dynamic Graphics (top left; middle right), Jupiter images / Liquid library (middle left, bottom left); **page 37** Dynamic Graphics; **page 38** Lonely Planet Images, *Greg Gawlowski* (left), **John Hay** (right); **page 39** Dynamic Graphics (right; middle left; bottom), Jupiter images / Liquid library (top left, top below, middle right); **page 40** Lonely Planet Images, *Karen Su*; **page 41** Lonely Planet Images, *Greg Caine*; **page 42** Lonely Planet Images, *Anders Blomqvist* (bottom), *Diana Mayfield* (top); **page 43** Lonely Planet Images, *Jon Davison* (left), *John Elk III* (right); **page 45** Jupiter images / Liquid library; **page 46** Corbis images; **page 47** Jupiter images / Liquid library; **page 49** Jupiter images / Liquid library; **page 51** Jupiter images / Liquid library; **page 52** Dynamic Graphics; **page 53** Jupiter images / Liquid library; **page 55** Jupiter images / Liquid library; **page 56** Library of Congress / *Sarony & Majors*; **page 57** Library of Congress / *John Trumbull*.